Pillars OF THE Almighty

Text **Ken Follett**
Photographs **f-stop Fitzgerald**

Introduction by Simon Verity

A BALLIETT & FITZGERALD BOOK

William Morrow and Company, Inc. • New York

Library of Congress Cataloging-in-Publication Data

Follett, Ken.
        [Pillars of the earth. Selections]
        Pillars of the Almighty / text by Ken Follett; photographs,
    f-stop Fitzgerald; introduction by Simon Verity.
            p.   cm.
        Excerpts from the novel, Pillars of the earth, by Ken Follett and photos of cathedrals.
        Includes index.
        ISBN 0-688-12812-2
        1. Cathedrals—Design and construction—Fiction. 2. Cathedrals—Pictorial works. I. Fitzgerald, f-stop. II. Title.
    PR6056.045P552   1994
    823' .914—dc20   94-5145
                        CIP

Printed in Japan

First Edition

1 2 3 4 5 6 7 8 9 10

Introduction

by Simon Verity
Master Sculptor at Cathedral of St. John the Divine

I come as an impostor to the stone trade from a family of architects. But, over the last thirty years, I have breathed enough dust and have taken as much abuse about the chips from my hair finding their way into the bed as any honest stoneman.

The best stonecutters are from uncomplicated rural stock, as stone is as much part of the life of the earth as farming. They're a breed apart, independent and truculent. Squaring a block, making it true, each step measured and with no shortcuts, gives a logic to the turn of the mind. It is no surprise to me that Socrates was a stonecutter.

New Age thinking about the properties of stone is anything but new; stonecutters have been swapping stories about strange stones and how to work them for thousands of years. They live and breathe this stuff, feeling out the different subtleties with their chisels. You can get a better paying job but you never get over stone once you have had it in your life. I once spent sixteen hours straight talking limestones and tools with a friend. The strange smell of a carboniferous limestone when you hit it. Is that

ure can be read clearly from below, no exaggerated muscles—they'd look like a bunch of sausages. See how the cutting is shallower where the strong south light hits it, deeper for the less intense east and west. Look at the simplicity of planes; look at the drawing in the gesture of that hand; that drapery is like a thirteenth-century molding." He showed me the connections that have fed my imagination ever since.

So I learnt and was able to earn a living doing this work. Hey, I even carved a naked full-sized statue ninety feet up on the venerable facade of Exeter Cathedral.

In late 1988, I got called in to play here, on St. John the Divine. Why an Englishman? Well, if you build a Gothic cathedral in America, you call in the English or the French, as we have a six-hundred-year-old church in every village. And the French are impossible as we all know . . .

The interior of this huge, glorious building has an extraordinary holiness that ebbs and flows. The exterior is flawed, ponderous, over-detailed and unfinished. But for me here are twelve eight-foot-high blocks of fine Indiana limestone waiting to be carved into prophets. Nothing like this is going on in Europe. It's all "new wine in old bottles" there. The endless tradition. I was talking to a friend who was apprenticed at Oxford and his respect for the ancient stonemason who taught him was almost Zen-like. This octogenarian had had half his hand blown off in the First World War, but with a chisel tied to it could cut a straighter line than anyone in the yard. I, myself, use the same arc-shaped hammer as I have seen depicted in the mason's stained glass window at Chartres dating from the thirteenth century.

Iron hammer. Lead dummy. Wooden mallet. Hard and soft striking tools have been used on stone since Neolithic man cracked flints with a stone hammer and pared them with a softer antler head. Our applewood mallets are carefully chosen with a truncated branch to withstand the endless beating on the steel tools. To strike on the wrong "beat" of the mallet will destroy it, so a favorite will never be lent.

My home was in the superb limestone hills around Bath. I would come across old men sawing the soft stone with a long handsaw, rocking to and fro on a single-legged stool, to be worked into a huge shell carving to go over a doorway. There, in the open air with only bars and rollers to maneuver the huge blocks. The quarrying underground was so hard that men would give up and die in their thirties, or would keep going out of sheer cussed willpower into their nineties. Until a few years ago it was all handpick and six-foot handsaw. Stories of a harsh code are legion.

the trapped smell from millions of years ago when the minute remains of plant life were rotting as they slowly turned to mud? How you dream of a stone when you see how it works, how another is so incredibly beautiful, how to work it easily, coax and tame each in such individual ways, because of their differing characteristics. You have to face it; it's a love affair, but bittersweet; you hate it sometimes, so remorselessly heavy, so hard and unyielding, yet so fragile.

I worked in England on cathedrals for years; six weeks on my knees in Canterbury, inlaying an inscription to mark the site of the Shrine of Thomas à Becket. At night I was shut in with all the ghosts of princes, kings and queens, pilgrims and stonecutters with just a single beam of light on my work. Awesome.

Wells was another, with the best thirteenth-century sculpture anywhere, and the best teacher to open my eyes to them. "Search for simplicity, for legibility, so that the fig-

Fingers mangled by a cog in the hoist? "Wrap it up and use your other hand," says the foreman. One of my mates was cut in half by the fall of a quarry crane.

Now I trudge through the derelict streets of Harlem to the cathedral, my tools over my shoulder. It's a medieval horizon on the hill, massive, somber, squat with its unfinished towers. Here is my doorway facing west, my work laid out before me with the imperfections, the experiments, the hope, the possibilities. There is now no man alive who has the same experience I have, has worked this particular way. I am tracing painfully, intuitively, the same wellspring that gave life to a medieval maker of images. The flimsy scaffolding is kept as free of boards as possible for me to look through and up at the half-worked figures behind. Is the silhouette strong? Does it read from across the street? Having the blocks upright gives you a clearer sense of the relationship of one statue to the next. But medieval statues were carved nearly horizontally before

being put in place, so that you could stand back and eye how it would be when sixty feet higher. Here we curse as we bang our knuckles trying to carve down the backs of the vertical stones, stopping only to remove chips of stone from our eyes—with the single hair of a brush twisted into a loop—as we pick upwards to hollow under drapery. I climb up and shake hands with Jean-Claude. How does he get up so early after such drinking sessions? Half my age, he has taught me so much. The French concentration is ferocious, and nothing is too difficult for him. From a family of stonecutters, he can visualize how the finished work will look at a glance and has an instinctive grasp of the tools to get him there. Now he picks up a chemin de fer, a stone plane that screams as it scrapes through the stone to finish a hollow in a piece of drapery. Only the French would invent such an infernal tool. I spit on my hump of sandstone and start to sharpen my tools. Working in a workshop with pneumatic tools around him

is difficult for a Frenchman, as he is used to listening. The sound of his hammer on his punch will tell him if he is going too deep and automatically he will drop his hand to lower the angle. Sebastian, who worked here two seasons past, had thick velvet pants that the dust fell from at the end of a day, with a pocket to hold a bottle of wine—a standard feature in Dijon. I once showed him how effective a stiff brush was for indicating with paint where shadows were needed and explained that they must have used the same tool a thousand years ago. "Oh, but for fine lines you paint with a feather," he said. It works. This must be the unbroken medieval French tradition, and I think of the crisp clarity of early moldings drawn with the lightness of a feather.

I was once working in a quarry fifty yards from the sea in Dorset, when the quarry master said, "Come with me to see where we got the marble for Salisbury Cathedral." So he drove me to the overgrown workings, and I asked him to show me where he was digging for the Purbeck marble. "Ah," he said, "the Lady of the Manor of Downshay gave the marble from her land here in 1220." To dig stone on the Isle of Purbeck you have to be the son of a quarryman; the sense of continuity is intense.

But the French training as campagnons is more medieval than the English. They may start at fourteen and will lead a semi-monastic life for years. Jean-Claude had his hair shoved into setting plaster because it was too long. They travel extensively to get a grasp of different aspects of the trade so that by their twenties they are superb craftsmen, even if arrogance keeps them from learning what they could from foreigners. After several years, Jean-Claude rebelled from the enclosed, rigorous life of a compagnon: "I must have a life, Simon." Life for him is very simple, either something is alive or it is dead. If a drawing is finished, or a tool will not keep an edge, for him it is "dead."

So we sit on our single board high in the air, the simple tools laid out between us. A pitcher to crack off fist-size lumps, then a punch for a series of troughs to lift off a line of stone along the grain; a claw to plow brittle stone without "plucking"; a chisel to flatten and round the forms of this fine-grained stone.

We hammer away with discipline and patience, and slowly the work comes together. But it is not straightforward. A little taken from a drapery by the shin affects the balance, perhaps a deeper hollow by the other shoulder. Balancing shadows, connections of lines, keeping an angle that will "read" from below; you search for a musical harmonic.

Our viewpoint of the street from the scaffolding is the best in the world, the most pluralist collection of races because of Columbia University: the rich, the poor. There is a connection with every other cathedral in the world that is a pilgrimage site and a connection with medieval stories. The poverty, the beggars; the girl who abandons her baby in the Cathedral and runs away; the young man who watches me work for four days without moving from the steps and is later found dead at the gate; Clyde, who in putting up netting to stop the nesting pigeons falls from a fifty-foot scaffold and, as in a truly medieval miracle, lives still. The distractions of tourists, the bone-chilling feel of a chisel in your hand in December, the dust and pigeon dung blowing endlessly in your eyes in the fall winds—all these stonecutters have known from time immemorial.

So we hammer and scrape smooth, keep an eye out for beautiful girls, live and breathe this extraordinary life that stone gives us, with its dreams of unimaginable eons of time when it was primeval ooze, compressed marine life that makes up a limestone and that no one has ever seen before until we open it up. Yes, there are dangers, but what other life is there for a man?

Jean-Claude and I are a fragile link in a chain that will include some extraordinary stonecutters as yet unborn as well as those past. We scratch away on the doorway to this great leviathan of a building, connected to its life through the bond with the body of men needed over its hundred-year life to construct it, and to the wider world of bishops, deans, financiers, pilgrims.

My family originally hailed from Beauvais, a city in northern France famous for its cathedral. This had the highest nave ever built in medieval times, but it collapsed. They had reached too high. Like the space programs after Challenger exploded, medieval builders stopped experimenting and worked within safer limits. The wildness was gone. I am glad to be part of another brave experiment with our imperfect striving for perfection. Who knows if cathedrals will become again the focus of the human spirit. But sometimes if I turn around I see the yearning face of some young man watching us work. And I know there will always be stonecutters.

By
Ken Follett

He had worked on a cathedral once—
Exeter. At first he had treated it like any
other job. He had been angry and resentful
when the master builder had warned him
that his work was not quite up to standard:
he knew himself to be rather more careful
than the average mason. But then he realized
that the walls of a cathedral had to be not
just good, but *perfect*. This was because the
cathedral was for God, and also because the
building was so *big* that the slightest lean in
the walls, the merest variation from the
absolutely true and level, could weaken the
structure fatally. Tom's resentment turned to
fascination. The combination of a hugely
ambitious building with merciless attention to
the smallest detail opened Tom's eyes to the
wonder of his craft. He learned from the
Exeter master about the importance of proportion, the symbolism of various numbers,
and the almost magical formulas for working
out the correct width of a wall or the angle
of a step in a spiral staircase. Such things cap-
tivated him. He was surprised to learn that
many masons found them incomprehensible.

His wife, Agnes, had never understood . . .
She could not comprehend the irresistible
attraction of building a cathedral: the absorbing complexity of organization, the intellectual challenge of the calculations, the sheer
size of the walls, and the breathtaking beauty
and grandeur of the finished building. Once
he had tasted that wine, Tom was never satisfied with anything less.

As he walked Tom thought about the cathedral he would build one day. He began, as always, by picturing an archway. It was very simple: two uprights supporting a semicircle. Then he imagined a second, just the same as the first. He pushed the two together, in his mind, to form one deep archway. Then he added another, and another, then a lot more, until he had a whole row of them, all stuck together, forming a tunnel. This was the essence of a building, for it had a roof to keep the rain off and two walls to hold up the roof. A church was just a tunnel, with refinements.

A tunnel was dark, so the first refinements were windows. If the wall was strong enough, it could have holes in it. The holes would be round at the top, with straight sides and a flat sill—the same shape as the original archway. Using similar shapes for arches and windows and doors was one of the things that made a building beautiful. Regularity was another, and Tom visualized twelve identical windows, evenly spaced, along each wall of the tunnel.

Tom tried to visualize the moldings over the windows, but his concentration kept slipping because he had the feeling that he was being watched. It was a foolish notion, he thought, if only because of course he *was* being observed by the birds, foxes, cats, squirrels, rats, mice, weasels, stoats and voles which thronged the forest.

Tom wondered what Salisbury cathedral would be like. A cathedral was a church like any other, in principle: it was simply the church where the bishop had his throne. But in practice cathedral churches were the biggest, richest, grandest and most elaborate. A cathedral was rarely a tunnel with windows. Most were three tunnels, a tall one flanked by two smaller ones in a head-and-shoulders shape, forming a nave with side aisles. The side walls of the central tunnel were reduced to two lines of pillars linked by arches, forming an arcade. The aisles were used for processions—which could be spectacular in cathedral churches—and might also provide space for small side chapels dedicated to particular saints, which attracted important extra donations. Cathedrals were the most costly buildings in the world, far more so than palaces or castles, and they had to earn their keep.

Salisbury was closer than Tom had thought. Around mid-morning they crested a rise, and found the road falling away gently before them in a long curve; and across the rainswept fields, rising out of the flat plain like a boat on a lake, they saw the fortified hill town of Salisbury. Its details were veiled by the rain, but Tom could make out several towers, four or five, soaring high above the city walls. His spirits lifted at the sight of so much stonework.

They were inside the walled cathedral close, which occupied the entire northwest quarter of the circular town. Tom stood for a moment taking it in. Just seeing and hearing and smelling it gave him a thrill like a sunny day. As they arrived behind the cartload of stone, two more carts were leaving empty. In lean-to sheds all along the side walls of the church, masons could be seen sculpting the stone blocks, with iron chisels and big wooden hammers, into the shapes that would be put together to form plinths, columns, capitals, shafts, buttresses, arches, windows, sills, pinnacles, and parapets. In the middle of the close, well away from other buildings, stood the smithy, the glow of its fire visible through the open doorway; and the clang of hammer on anvil carried across the close as the smith made new tools to replace the ones the masons were wearing down. To most people it was a scene of chaos, but Tom saw a large and complex mechanism which he itched to control. He knew what each man was doing and he could see instantly how far the work had progressed. They were building the east facade.

There was a run of scaffolding across the east end at a height of twenty-five or thirty feet. The masons were in the porch, waiting for the rain to ease up, but their laborers were running up and down the ladders with stones on their shoulders. Higher up, on the timber framework of the roof, were the plumbers, like spiders creeping across a giant wooden web, nailing sheets of lead to the struts and installing the drainpipes and gutters.

Tom realized regretfully that the building was almost finished. If he did get hired here the work would not last more than a couple of years—hardly enough time for him to rise to the position of master mason, let alone master builder. Nevertheless he would take the job, if he were offered it, for winter was coming. He and his family could have survived winter without work if they had still had the pig, but without it Tom had to get a job.

He arrived at the cathedral close without seeing the outlaw. He looked at the plumbers nailing the lead to the triangular timber roof over the nave. They had not yet begun to cover the lean-to roofs on the side aisles of the church, and it was still possible to see the supporting half-arches which connected the outside edge of the aisle with the main nave wall, propping up the top half of the church. He pointed them out to Alfred.

"Without those supports, the nave wall would bow outward and buckle, because of the weight of the stone vaults inside," he explained. "See how the half-arches line up with the buttresses in the aisle wall? And the aisle windows line up with the arches of the arcade. Strong lines up with strong, and weak with weak." Alfred looked baffled and resentful. Tom sighed.

From where he lay Tom could see the towers of the cathedral. He wished he had had a moment to look inside. He was curious about the treatment of the piers of the arcade. These were usually fat pillars, each with arches sprouting from its top: two arches going north and south, to connect with the neighboring pillars in the arcade; and one going east or west, across the side aisle. It was an ugly effect, for there was something not quite right about an arch that sprang from the top of a round column. When Tom built his cathedral each pier would be a cluster of shafts, with an arch springing from the top of each shaft—an elegantly logical arrangement.

He began to visualize the decoration of the arches. Geometric shapes were the commonest forms—it did not take much skill to carve zigzags and lozenges—but Tom liked foliage, which lent softness and a touch of nature to the hard regularity of the stones.

L ike most churches, Kingsbridge Cathedral was built in the shape of a cross. The west end opened into the nave, which formed the long stem of the cross. The crosspiece consisted of the two transepts which stuck out to the north and south either side of the altar. Beyond the crossing, the east end of the church was called the chancel, and was mainly reserved for the monks. At the farthest extremity of the east end was the tomb of Saint Adolphus, which still attracted occasional pilgrims.

Philip stepped into the nave and looked down the avenue of round arches and mighty columns. The sight further depressed his mood. It was a dank, gloomy building, and it had deteriorated since he last saw it. The windows in the low aisles either side of the nave were like narrow tunnels in the immensely thick walls. Up in the roof, the larger windows of the clerestory illuminated the painted timber ceiling only to show how badly it was fading, the apostles and saints and prophets growing dim and blending inexorably with their background. Despite the cold air blowing in—for there was no glass in the windows—a faint smell of rotting vestments tainted the atmosphere. From the other end of the church came the sound of the service of high mass, the Latin phrases spoken in a singsong voice, and the chanted responses. Philip walked down the nave. The floor had never been paved, so moss grew on the bare earth in the corners where peasant clogs and monkish sandals rarely trod. The carved spirals and flutes of the massive columns, and the incised chevrons that decorated the arches between them, had once been painted and gilded; but now all that remained were a few flakes of papery gold leaf and a patchwork of stains where the paint had been. The mortar between the stones was crumbling and falling out, and gathering in little heaps by the walls. Philip felt a familiar anger rise in him again. When people came here they were supposed to be awestruck by the majesty of Almighty God. But peasants were simple people who judged by appearances, and coming here they would like to think that God was a careless, indifferent deity unlikely to appreciate their worship or take note of their sins. In the end the peasants paid for the church with the sweat of their brows, and it was outrageous that they were rewarded with this crumbling mausoleum.

The eastern arm of the church, the chancel, was divided into two. Nearest the crossing was the quire, with wooden stalls where the monks sat and stood during the services. Beyond the quire was the sanctuary that housed the tomb of the saint. Philip moved behind the alter, intending to take a place in the quire; then he was brought up short by a coffin.

Kingsbridge Cathedral was not a welcoming sight. It was a low, squat, massive structure with thick walls and tiny windows. It had been built long before Tom's time, in the days when builders had not realized the importance of proportion. Tom's generation knew that a straight, true wall was stronger than a thick one, and that walls could be pierced with large windows so long as the arch of the window was a perfect half-circle. From a distance the church looked lopsided, and when Tom got closer he saw why: one of the twin towers at the west end had fallen down. He was delighted. The new prior was likely to want it rebuilt. Hope quickened his

pace. To have been hired, as he had been at Earlcastle, and then to see his new employer defeated in battle and captured was heartbreaking. He felt he could not take another disappointment like that.

He glanced at Ellen. He was afraid that any day now she would decide that he was not going to find work before they all starved to death, and then she would leave him. She smiled at him, then she frowned again as she looked at the looming bulk of the cathedral. She was always uncomfortable with priests and monks, he had observed. He wondered if she felt guilty because the two of them were not actually married in the eyes of the Church.

❖

He hesitated under the arch, looking into the moonlit quadrangle. There must be a way to sneak into such a big building, he felt, but he could not think where else to look. In a way he was glad. He had been contemplating doing something appallingly dangerous, and it if turned out to be impossible, so much the better. On the other hand, he dreaded the thought of leaving this priory and taking to the road again in the morning: the endless walking, the hunger, Tom's disappointment and anger, Martha's tears. It could all be

avoided, just by one little spark from the flint he carried in the little pouch hanging from his belt!

Something moved at the corner of his vision. He started, and his heart beat faster. He turned his head and saw, to his horror, a ghostly figure, carrying a candle, gliding silently along the east walk toward the church. A scream rose in his throat and he fought it down. Another figure followed the first. Jack stepped back into the archway, out of sight, and put his fist in his mouth, biting his skin to stop himself from crying aloud. He heard an eerie moaning sound. He stared in sheer terror. Then realization dawned: what he was seeing was a procession of monks going from the dormitory to the church for the midnight service, singing a hymn as they went. The panicky feeling persisted for a moment, even when he had understood what he was looking at; then relief washed over him, and he began to shake uncontrollably.

The monk at the head of the procession unlocked the door to the church with a huge iron key. The monks filed in. No one turned around to look in Jack's direction. Most of them appeared to be half asleep. They did not close the church door behind them.

When he had recovered his composure Jack realized that now he could get into the church.

His legs felt too weak to walk.

I could just go in, he thought. I don't have to do anything when I'm inside. I'll look and see whether it is possible to get up to the roof. I might not set fire to it. I'll just take a look.

He took a deep breath, then stepped out of the archway and padded across the quadrangle. He hesitated at the open door and peeped in. There were candles on the altar, and in the quire where the monks stood in their stalls, but the light merely made small pools in the middle of the big empty space, leaving the walls and the aisles in deep gloom. One of the monks was doing something incomprehensible at the altar, and the others would occasionally chant a few phrases of mumbo jumbo. It seemed incredible to Jack that people should get up out of warm beds in the middle of the night to do something like this.

He slipped through the door and stood close to the wall.

He was inside. The darkness concealed him.

❖

He peeped around the pillar. Above the altar, where the candles were brightest, he could just make out the high wooden ceiling. Newer churches had stone vaults, he knew, but Kingsbridge was old. That wooden ceiling would burn well.

I'm not going to do it, he thought.

At last he came out from behind his pillar.

He walked up the nave. It was an odd feeling, to be alone in this big, cold, empty building. This is what it must be like to be a mouse, he thought, hiding in corners when the big people are around and then coming out when they have gone. He reached the altar and took the fat, bright candle, and that made him feel better.

Carrying the candle, he began to inspect the inside of the church. At the corner where the nave met the south transept, the place where he had most feared being spotted by the monk at the altar, there was a door in the wall with a simple latch. He tried the latch. The door opened.

His candle revealed a spiral staircase, so narrow that a fat man could not have passed through it, so low that Tom would have had to bend double. He went up the steps.

He emerged in a narrow gallery. On one side, a row of small arches looked out into the nave. The ceiling sloped from the tops of the arches down to the floor on the other side. It took Jack a moment to realize where he was. He was above the aisle on the south side of the nave. The tunnel-vaulted ceiling of the aisle was the curved floor on which Jack was standing. From the outside of the

church the aisle could be seen to have a lean-to roof, and that was the sloping ceiling under which Jack was standing. The aisle was much lower than the nave, so he was still a long way from the main roof of the building.

He walked west along the gallery, exploring. It was quite thrilling, now that the monks had gone and he was no longer in fear of being spotted. It was as if he had climbed a tree and found that at the very top, hidden from view by the lower branches, all the trees were connected, and you could walk around in a secret world a few feet above the earth.

At the end of the gallery was another small door. He went through it and found himself on the inside of the southwest tower, the one that had not fallen down. The space he was in was obviously not meant to be seen, for it was rough and unfinished, and instead of a floor there were rafters with wide gaps between them. However, around the inside of the wall ran a flight of wooden steps, a staircase without a handrail. Jack went up.

Halfway up one wall was a small arched opening. The staircase passed right by it. Jack put his head inside and held up his candle. He was in the roof space, above the timber ceiling and below the lead roof.

At first he could see no pattern in the tangle of wooden beams, but after a moment he perceived the structure. Huge oak timbers, each of them a foot wide and two feet deep, spanned the width of the nave from north to south. Above each beam were two mighty rafters, forming a triangle; the regular row of triangles stretched away beyond the light of the candle. Looking down, between the beams, he could see the back of the painted wooden ceiling of the nave, which was fixed to the lower edges of the cross-beams.

At the edge of the roof space, in the corner at the base of the triangle, was a catwalk.

Jack crawled through the little opening and onto the catwalk. There was just enough headroom for him to stand up: a man would have had to stoop. He walked along it a little way. There was enough timber here for a conflagration. He sniffed, trying to identify the odd smell in the air. He decided it was pitch. The roof timbers were tarred. They would burn like straw.

A sudden movement on the floor startled him and made his heart race. He thought of the headless knight in the river and the ghostly monks in the cloisters. Then he thought of mice, and felt better. But when he looked carefully he saw that it was birds: there were nests under the eaves.

The roof space followed the pattern of the church below, branching out over the transepts. Jack went as far as the crossing and stood at the corner. He realized he must be directly above the little spiral staircase that had brought him from ground level up to the gallery. If he had been planning to start a fire, this was where he would do it. From here it could spread four ways: west along the nave, south along the south transept, and through the crossing to the chancel and the north transept.

The main timbers of the roof were made of heart-of-oak, and although they were tarred they might not catch fire from a candle flame. However, under the eaves was a litter of ancient wood chips and shavings, discarded bits of rope and sacking, and abandoned birds' nests, which would make perfect kindling. All he would have to do would be to collect it and pile it up.

His candle was burning low.

It seemed so easy. Collect up the litter, touch the candle flame to it, and leave. Cross the close like a ghost, slip into the guesthouse, bar the door, curl up in the straw and wait for the alarm.

But if he were seen . . .

If he should be caught now, he could say he was harmlessly exploring the cathedral, and he would suffer no worse than a spanking. But if they caught him setting fire to the church they would do more than spank him. He remembered the sugar thief in Shiring, and the way his bottom bled. He recalled some of the punishments the outlaws had suffered: Faramond Openmouth had had his lips cut off, Jack Flathat had lost his hand, and Alan Catface had been put in the stocks and stoned and had never been able to talk properly since. Even worse were the stories of those who had not survived their punishments: a murderer who had been tied to a barrel studded with spikes and then rolled downhill so that all the spikes went through his body; a horse thief who had been burned alive; a thieving whore who had been impaled on a pointed stake. What would they do to a boy who set fire to a church?

Thoughtfully, he began to collect the inflammable rubbish from under the eaves and pile it up on the catwalk exactly below one of the mighty rafters.

When he had a pile a foot high he sat down and looked at it.

His candle guttered. In a few moments he

would have lost his chance.

With a quick motion he touched the candle flame to a piece of sacking. It caught fire. The flame spread immediately to some wood shavings, then a dried, crumbling bird's nest; and then the little fire was blazing cheerfully.

I could still put it out, Jack thought.

The kindling was burning a little too quickly: at this rate it would be used up before the roof timber began to smolder. Jack hurriedly collected more rubbish and piled it on. The flames rose higher. I could still put it out, he thought. The pitch with which the beam was coated began to blacken and smoke. The rubbish burned up. I could just let the fire go out, now, he thought. Then he saw that the catwalk itself was burning. I could probably smother the fire with my cloak, still, he thought. Instead he threw more litter onto the fire and watched it burn higher.

The atmosphere became hot and smoky in the little angle of the eaves, even though the freezing night air was only an inch away on the other side of the roof. Some of the smaller timbers, to which the lead sheets of the roof were nailed, began to burn. Then, at last, a small flame flickered up from the massive main beam.

The cathedral was on fire.

It was done now. There was no turning back.

Jack felt scared. Suddenly he wanted to get out fast, and return to the guesthouse. He wanted to be rolled up in his cloak, nestling in a little hollow in the straw, with his eyes shut tight, and the others breathing evenly all around him. He retreated along the catwalk.

When he reached the end he looked back. The fire was spreading surprisingly quickly, perhaps because of the pitch with which the wood was coated. All the small timbers were ablaze, the main beams were beginning to burn, and the fire was spreading along the catwalk. Jack turned his back on it.

He ducked into the tower and went down the stairs, then ran along the gallery over the aisle and hurried down the spiral staircase to the floor of the nave. He ran to the door by which he had come in.

It was locked.

He realized he had been stupid. The monks had unlocked the door when they came in, so of course they had locked it again as they left.

Fear rose in his throat like bile. He had set the church on fire and now he was locked inside. He fought down panic and tried to think. He had tried every door from the outside, and found them all locked; but perhaps some of them were fastened with bars, rather than locks, so that they could be opened from the inside.

He hurried across the crossing to the north transept and examined the door in the north porch. It had a lock.

He ran down the dark nave to the west end and tried each of the great public entrances. All three doors were locked with keys. Finally he tried the little door that led into the south aisle from the north walk of the cloister square. That, too, was locked.

Jack wanted to cry, but that would do no good. He looked up at the wooden ceiling. Was it his imagination, or could he see, by the faint moonlight, a little smoke drifting out from the ceiling near the corner of the south transept?

He thought: What am I going to do?

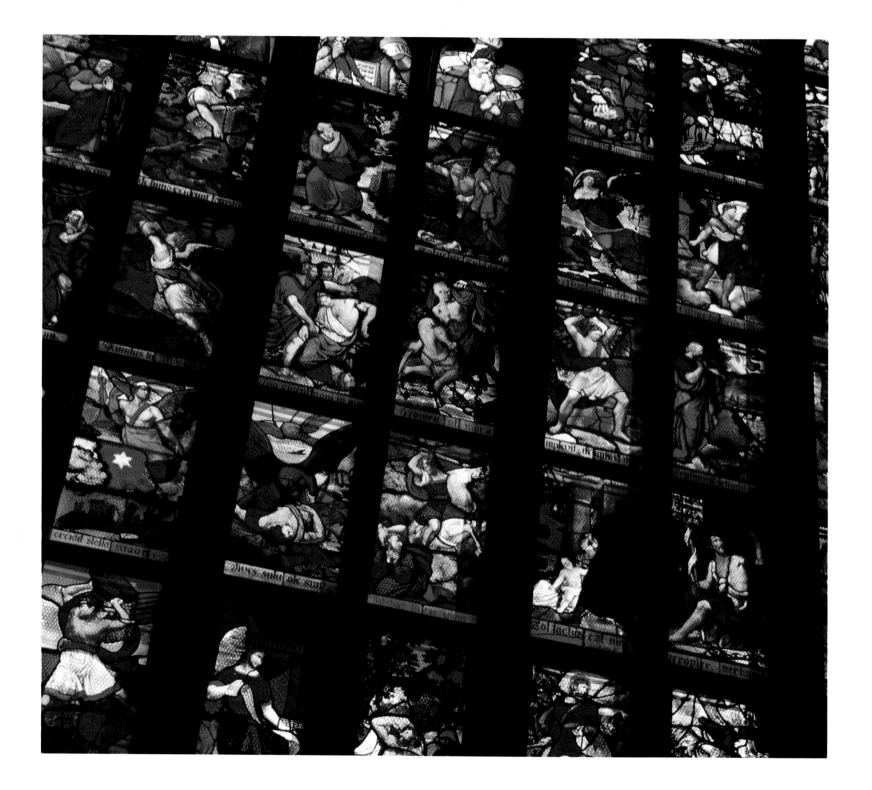

Would the monks wake up, and come rushing in to put out the fire, in such a panic that they hardly noticed one small boy slipping out through the door? Or would they see him immediately, and grab him, screaming accusations? Or would they stay asleep, all unconscious, until the whole building had collapsed, and Jack lay crushed under a huge pile of stones?

Tears came to his eyes, and he wished he had never touched the candle flame to that pile of litter.

He looked around wildly. If he went to a window and screamed, would anybody hear?

There was a crash from above. He looked up and saw that a hole had appeared in the wooden ceiling, where a beam had fallen and poked through. The hole appeared as a patch of red on a black background. A moment later there was another crash, and a huge timber smashed right through the ceiling and fell, turning over once in the air, to hit the ground with a thump that shook the mighty columns of the nave. A shower of sparks and burning embers drifted down after it. Jack listened, waiting for shouts, cries for help, or the ringing of a bell; but nothing happened. The crash had not been heard. And if that had not awakened them, they certainly would not hear him screaming.

I'm going to die here, he thought hysterically; I'm going to burn or be crushed, unless I can think of a way out!

He thought of the fallen tower. He had examined it from the outside, and he had not seen a way in, but then he had been timid, for fear of falling and causing a landslide. Perhaps if he looked again, from the inside this time, he would see something he had missed; and perhaps desperation would help him squeeze through where before he had seen no gap.

He ran to the west end. The glow of the fire coming through the hole in the ceiling, combined with the flames licking up from the beam that had fallen to the floor of the nave,

now gave stronger light than the moon, and the arcade of the nave was edged with gold instead of silver. Jack examined the pile of stones that had once been the northwest tower. They appeared to form a solid wall. There was no way through. Foolishly, he opened his mouth and yelled "Mother!" at the top of his voice, even though he knew she could not hear.

He fought down his panic once again. There was something in the back of his mind about this collapsed tower. He had been able to get inside the other tower, the one that was still standing, by going along the gallery over the south aisle. If he now went along the gallery over the north aisle, he might see a gap in the pile of rubble, a gap that was not visible from the ground level.

He ran back to the crossing, staying under the shelter of the north aisle in case more burning beams should come crashing through the ceiling. There should be a little door and a spiral staircase on this side, just as there was on the other. He came to the corner of the nave and the north transept. He could not see the door. He looked around the corner: it was not on the other side either. He could not believe his bad luck. It was crazy: there had to be a way into the gallery!

He thought hard, fighting to stay calm. There was a way into the fallen tower, he just had to find it. I could get back into the roof space, via the good, southwest tower, he thought. I could cross to the other side of the roof space. There should be a little opening on that side, giving access to the collapsed northwest tower. That may provide me with a way out.

He looked up at the ceiling fearfully. The fire would be an inferno. But he could not think of any alternative.

First he had to cross the nave. He looked up again. As far as he could tell, there was nothing about to come down immediately. He took a deep breath and dashed across to the other side. Nothing fell on him.

In the south aisle, he pulled open the little door and ran up the spiral staircase. When he reached the top and stepped into the gallery he could feel the warmth of the fire above. He ran along the gallery, went through the door into the good tower, and raced up the stairs.

He ducked his head and crawled through the little arch into the roof space. It was full of smoke and heat. All the uppermost timbers were ablaze, and at the far end the biggest beams were burning strongly. The tarry smell made Jack cough. He hesitated only a moment, then stepped onto one of the big beams that spanned the nave and began to walk across. In moments he was wet with perspiration because of the heat, and his eyes began to water so that he could hardly see where he was going. He coughed, and then his foot slipped off the beam and he stumbled sideways. He fell with one foot on the beam and one foot off. His right foot landed on the ceiling, and to his horror it went straight through the rotted wood. A picture flashed into his mind of the height of the nave, and how far he would drop if he fell right through the ceiling; and he screamed as he tumbled forward, putting his arms out in front of him, imagining himself turning over and over in the air as the falling beam had done. But the wood held his weight.

He remained frozen still, shocked, resting on his hands and one knee, with the other leg sticking through the ceiling. Then the fierce heat of the fire brought him out of his shock. Gently he extracted his foot from the hole. He got on his hands and knees and crawled forward.

As he neared the other side, several large beams fell into the nave. The whole building seemed to shake, and the beam under Jack quivered like a bowstring. He stopped and held on tight. The tremor passed. He crawled on, and a moment later he reached the catwalk on the north side.

If his guess turned out to be wrong, and there was no opening from here into the ruins of the northwest tower, he would have to go back.

As he stood upright, he got a breath of cold night air. There must be some kind of gap. But would it be big enough for a small boy?

He took three paces to the west and stopped an instant before he would have stepped out into nothingness.

He found himself looking through a large hole out onto the moonlit ruins of the fallen tower. His knees went weak with relief. He was out of the inferno.

But he was high up, at roof level, and the top of the rubble pile was a long way below him, too far to jump. He could escape the flames now, but could he reach the ground without breaking his neck? Behind him, the flames were rapidly coming closer, and smoke was billowing out of the opening in which he stood.

This tower had once had a staircase around its inner wall, just as the other one still did, but most of this staircase had been destroyed in the collapse. However, where the wooden treads had been set into the wall with mortar, there were stumps of wood sticking out, sometimes just an inch or two long, sometimes more. Jack wondered whether he could climb down the stumps. It would be a precarious descent. He noticed a smell of scorching: his cloak was getting hot. In a moment it would catch fire. He had no choice.

He sat down, reached out for the nearest stump, held on with both hands, then eased one leg down until he found a foothold. Then he put the other foot down. Feeling his way with his feet, he eased himself down one step. The stumps held. He reached down once again, testing the strength of the next stump before putting his weight on it. This one felt a little loose. He trod gingerly, holding on tightly in case he should find himself swinging by his hands. Each perilous step brought him nearer to the top of the rubble pile. As he descended, the stumps seemed to get smaller, as if the lower ones had suffered more severe damage. He put one foot,

in its felt boot, on a stump no wider than his toe; and when he rested his weight on it his foot slipped. His other foot was on a larger stump, but when suddenly he put his full weight on it the other stump broke. He tried to hold on with his hands, but the stumps were so small that he could not grip hard, and he slipped, terrified, from his precarious perch and fell through the air.

He landed hard on his hands and knees on the top of the pile of rubble. For an instant he was so shocked and frightened he thought he must be dead; then he realized that he had been lucky enough to fall well. His hands stung and his knees would be massively bruised, but he was all right.

After a moment he climbed down the pile of rubble and jumped the last few feet to the ground.

He was safe. He felt weak with relief. He wanted to cry again. He had escaped. He felt proud: what an adventure he had had!

But it was not yet over. Out here there was only a whiff of smoke, and the noise of the fire, so deafening inside the roof space, now sounded like a distant wind. Only the reddish glow behind the windows proved that the church was on fire. Nevertheless, those last tremors must have disturbed someone's sleep, and any moment now a bleary-eyed monk would come stumbling out of the dormitory, wondering whether the earthquake he had felt had been real or only a dream. Jack had set fire to the church—a heinous crime in the eyes of a monk. He had to get away quickly.

He ran across the grass to the guesthouse. All was quiet and still. He stopped outside, panting. If he went in breathing like this he would wake them all. He tried to control his

breathing but that seemed to make it worse. He would just have to stay here until it became normal again.

A bell rang, piercing the quiet, and went on, pealing urgently, an unmistakable alarm. Jack froze. If he went inside now they would know. But if he did not—

The door of the guesthouse opened, and Martha came out. Jack just stared at her, terrified.

"Where have you been?" she said softly. "You smell of smoke."

A plausible lie came into Jack's head. "I've only just stepped out," he said desperately. "I heard that bell."

"Liar," Martha said. "You've been gone for ages. I know, I was awake."

He realized there was no fooling her. "Was anyone else awake?" he said fearfully.

"No, only me."

"Don't tell them I was gone. Please?"

She heard the fear in his voice and spoke soothingly. "All right, I'll keep it a secret. Don't worry."

"Thank you!"

At that moment Tom stepped out, scratching his head.

Jack was frightened. What would Tom think?

"What's going on?" Tom said sleepily. He sniffed. "I smell smoke."

Jack pointed at the cathedral with a trembling arm. "I think . . ." he said, and then swallowed. It was going to be all right, he realized, with a grateful sense of relief. Tom would just assume that Jack had got up a moment earlier, as Martha had. Jack spoke again, more confidently this time. "Look at the church," he said to Tom. "I think it's on fire."

H is reflections were interrupted again, this time by a louder bang that actually made his house shake slightly. That was definitely *not* a door slamming, he thought. Whatever is going on over there? He went to the window and opened the shutter. The cold night blew in, making him shiver. He looked out over the church, the chapter house, the cloisters, the dormitory and the kitchen buildings beyond. They all appeared peaceful in the moonlight. The air was so frosty that his teeth hurt when he breathed. But there was something else about the air. He sniffed. He could smell smoke.

He frowned anxiously, but he could see no fire.

He drew his head into the room and sniffed again, thinking that he might be smelling smoke from his own fireplace, but it was not so.

Mystified and alarmed, he pulled on his boots rapidly, picked up his cloak, and ran out of the house.

The smell of the smoke became stronger as he hurried across the green toward the cloisters. There was no doubt that some part of the priory was on fire. His first thought was that it must be the kitchen—nearly all fires started in kitchens. He ran through the passage between the south transept and the chapter house and across the cloister square. In daytime he would have gone through the refectory to the kitchen courtyard, but at night it was locked, so he went out through the arch in the south walk and turned right to the back of the kitchen. There was no sign of fire here, nor in the brewery or the bakehouse, and the smell of smoke now seemed a little less. He ran a little farther, and looked past the corner of the brewery, across the green to the guesthouse and the stables. All seemed quiet over there.

Could the fire be in the dormitory? The dormitory was the only other building with a fireplace. The thought was horrifying. As he ran back into the cloisters he had a grisly vision of all the monks in their beds, overcome by smoke, unconscious as the dormitory blazed. He ran to the dormitory door. As he reached it, it opened, and Cuthbert Whitehead stepped out, carrying a rushlight.

Cuthbert said immediately: "Can you smell it?"

"Yes—are the monks all right?"

"There's no fire here."

Philip was relieved. At least his flock was safe. "Where, then?"

"What about the kitchen?" Cuthbert said.

"No—I've checked." Now that he knew nobody was in danger, he began to worry about his property. He had just been thinking about finances, and he knew he could not afford repairs to buildings right now. He looked at the church. Was there a faint red glow behind the windows?

Philip said: "Cuthbert, get the church key from the sacrist."

Cuthbert was ahead of him. "I have it here."

"Good man!"

They hurried along the east walk to the door in the south transept. Cuthbert unlocked it hastily. As soon as the door swung open, smoke billowed out.

Philip's heart missed a beat. How could this church be on fire?

He stepped inside. At first the scene was confusing. On the floor of the church, around the altar and here in the south transept, several huge pieces of wood were burning. Where had they come from? How had they produced so much smoke? And what was the roaring noise that sounded like a much bigger fire?

Cuthbert shouted: "Look up!"

Philip looked up and his questions were answered. The ceiling was blazing furiously. He stared at it, horrified: it looked like the underside of hell. Most of the painted ceiling had already gone, revealing the timber triangles of the roof, blackened and blazing, the flames and smoke leaping and swirling in a fiendish dance. Philip stood still, shocked into immobility, until his neck started to hurt from looking up; then he gathered his wits.

He ran to the middle of the crossing, stood in front of the altar, and looked around the whole church. The entire roof was ablaze, from the west door to the east end and all across both transepts. For a panicky moment he thought *How are we going to get water up there?* He imagined a line of monks running along the gallery with buckets, and he realized immediately that it was impossible: even if he had a hundred people for the job, they could not carry up to the roof a quantity of water sufficient to put out this roaring inferno. The whole roof was going to be destroyed, he realized with a sinking heart; and the rain and snow would fall into the church until he could find the money for a new roof.

A crashing sound made him look up. Immediately above him an enormous timber was moving slowly sideways. It was going to fall on top of him. He dashed back into the south transept, where Cuthbert stood looking scared.

A whole section of the roof, three triangles of beam-and-rafter plus the lead sheets nailed to them, was falling in. Philip and Cuthbert watched, transfixed, quite forgetting their own safety. The roof fell on one of the big round arches of the crossing. The enormous weight of the falling wood and lead cracked the stonework of the arch with a prolonged explosive sound like thunder. Everything happened slowly: the beams fell slowly, the arch broke up slowly, and the smashed masonry fell slowly through the air. More roof beams came free, and then, with a noise like a long slow peal of thunder, a whole section of the north wall of the chancel shuddered and slid sideways into the north transept.

Philip was appalled. The sight of such a mighty building being destroyed was strangely shocking. It was like watching a mountain fall down or a river run dry: he had never really thought it could happen. He could hardly believe his eyes. It made him feel disoriented, and he did not know what to do.

Cuthbert was tugging at his sleeve. "Come out!" he yelled.

He had forgotten the saint.

At the far end of the church, beyond the bishop's throne, was the stone tomb of Saint Adolphus, an early English martyr. Inside the tomb was a wooden coffin containing the skeleton of the saint. Periodically the lid of the tomb was lifted to display the coffin. Adolphus was not as popular now as he had once been, but in the old days sick people had been miraculously cured by touching the tomb. A saint's remains could be a big attraction in a church, promoting worship and pilgrimages. They brought in so much money that, shamefully, it was not unknown for monks actually to steal holy relics from other churches. Philip had planned to revive interest in Adolphus. He had to save the skeleton.

He would need help to lift the lid of the tomb and carry the coffin. The sacrist should have thought about this, too. But he was nowhere to be seen. The next monk to emerge from the dormitory was Remigius, the haughty sub-prior. He would have to do. Philip called him over and said: "Help me rescue the bones of the saint."

Remigius's pale green eyes looked fearfully at the burning church, but after a moment's hesitation he followed Philip along the east walk and through the door.

❖

Philip groaned. Of course—the books. They were kept in a locked cupboard in the east cloister, next to the door of the chapter house, where the monks could get them during study periods. It would take a dangerously long time to empty the cupboard book by book. Perhaps a few strong youngsters could pick up the whole cupboard and carry it to safety. Philip looked around. The sacrist had chosen half a dozen monks to deal with the coffin, and they were already making their way across the green. Now Philip selected three young monks and three of the older novices, and told them to follow him.

He retraced his steps across the open space in front of the burning church. He was too tired to run. They passed between the mill and the brewery, and went around the back of the kitchen and refectory. Cuthbert Whitehead and the sacrist were organizing the removal of the coffin. Philip led his group along the passage that ran between the refectory and the dormitory and under the south archway into the cloisters.

He could feel the heat of the fire. The big book cupboard had carvings on its doors depicting Moses and the tablets of stone. Philip directed the young men to tip the cupboard forward and hoist it on their shoulders. They carried it around the cloisters to the south archway. There Philip paused and looked back while they went on. His heart filled with grief at the sight of the ruined church. There was less smoke and more flame now. Whole stretches of the roof had disappeared. As he watched, the roof over the crossing seemed to sag, and he realized it was going to go next. There was a thunderous crash, louder than anything that had gone before, and the roof of the south transept fell in. Philip felt a pain that was almost physical, as if his own body were burning. A moment later the wall of the transept seemed to bulge out over the cloisters. God help us, it's going to fall down, Philip thought. As the stonework began to crumble and scatter he realized it was falling toward him, and he turned to flee; but before he had taken three steps something hit the back of his head and he lost consciousness.

W hen everyone was busy again, Prior Philip walked away from the guesthouse, on his own, and headed for the church. Tom saw him and followed. This was his chance. If he could handle this right he could work here for years.

Philip stood staring at what had been the west end of the church, shaking his head sadly at the wreckage, looking as if it were his life that was in ruins. Tom stood beside him in silence. After a while Philip moved on, walking along the north side of the nave, through the graveyard. Tom walked with him, surveying the damage.

The north wall of the nave was still standing, but the north transept and part of the north wall of the chancel had fallen. The church still had an east end. They turned around the end and looked at the south side. Most of the south wall had come down and the south transept had collapsed into the cloisters. The chapter house was still standing.

They walked to the archway that led into the east walk of the cloisters. There they were halted by the pile of rubble. It looked a mess, but Tom's trained eye could see that the cloister walks themselves were not badly damaged, just buried under the fallen ruins. He climbed over the broken stones until he could see into the church. Just behind the altar there was a semi-concealed staircase that led down into the crypt. The crypt itself was beneath the quire. Tom peered in, studying the stone floor over the crypt for signs of cracking. He could see none. There was a good chance the crypt had survived intact. He would not tell Philip yet: he would save the news for a crucial moment.

Philip had walked on, around the back of the dormitory. Tom hurried to catch him. They found the dormitory unmarked. Going on, they found the other monastic buildings more or less unharmed: the refectory, the kitchen, the bakehouse and the brewery. Philip might have taken some consolation in that, but his expression remained glum.

THEY ENDED UP WHERE
THEY HAD STARTED, IN
FRONT OF THE RUINED
WEST END, HAVING
COMPLETED A FULL
CIRCUIT OF THE PRIORY
CLOSE WITHOUT SPEAK-
ING A WORD. PHILIP
SIGHED HEAVILY AND
BROKE THE SILENCE.
"THE DEVIL DID THIS."

Tom thought: This is my moment. He took a deep breath and said: "It might be God's work."

Philip looked up at him in surprise. "How so?"

Tom said carefully: "No one has been hurt. The books, the treasure and the bones of the saint were saved. Only the church has been destroyed. Perhaps God wanted a new church."

Philip smiled skeptically. "And I suppose God wanted you to build it." He was not too stunned to see that Tom's line of thought might be self-interested.

Tom stood his ground. "It may be so," he said stubbornly. "It was not the devil who sent a master builder here on the night the church burned down."

Philip looked away. "Well, there will be a new church, but I don't know when. And what am I to do meanwhile? How can the life of the monastery go on? All we're here for is worship and study."

Philip was deep in despair. This was the moment for Tom to offer him new hope. "My boy and I could have the cloisters cleared and ready for use in a week," he said, making his voice sound more confident than he felt.

Philip was surprised. "Could you?" Then his expression changed once more, and he looked defeated again. "But what will we use for a church?"

"What about the crypt? You can hold services there, couldn't you?"

"Yes—it would do very well."

"I'm sure the crypt is not badly damaged," Tom said. It was almost true: he was almost sure.

Philip was looking at him as if he were the angel of mercy.

"It won't take long to clear a path through the debris from the cloisters to the crypt stairs," Tom went on. "Most of the church on that side has been completely destroyed, which is fortunate, oddly enough, because it means there's no further danger from falling masonry. I'd have to survey the walls that are still standing, and it might be necessary to shore some of them up. Then they should be checked every day for cracks, and even so you ought not to enter the church in a gale." All of this was important, but Tom could see that Philip was not taking it in. What Philip wanted from Tom now was positive news, something to lift his spirits. And the way to get hired was to give him what he wanted. Tom changed his tone. "With some of your younger monks laboring for me, I could fix things up so that you're able to resume normal monastic life, after a fashion, within two weeks."

Philip was staring at him. "Two weeks?"

"Give me food and lodging for my family, and you can pay my wages when you have the money."

"You could give me back my priory in two weeks?" Philip repeated incredulously.

Tom was not sure he could, but if it took three no one would die of it. "Two weeks," he said firmly. "After that, we can knock down the remaining walls—that's a skilled job, mind you, if it's to be done safely—then clear the rubble, stacking the stones for reuse. Meanwhile we can plan the new cathedral." Tom held his breath. He had done his best. Surely Philip would hire him now!

Philip nodded, smiling for the first time. "I think God did send you," he said. "Let's have some breakfast, then we can start work."

Tom breathed a shaky sigh of relief. "Thank you," he said. There was a quaver in his voice that he could not quite control, but suddenly he did not care, and with a barely suppressed sob, he said: "I can't tell you how much it means to me."

❖

For the first time ever, it occurred to Philip to wonder how such large stones could be moved. They were certainly too big for a man to lift. He saw the answer immediately. A pair of poles were laid side by side on the ground, and a stone was rolled along until it rested across the poles. Then two people would take the ends of the poles and lift. Tom Builder must have shown them how to do that.

The work was proceeding rapidly, with most of the priory's sixty servants helping, making a stream of people carrying stones away and coming back for more. The sight lifted Philip's spirits, and he gave up a silent prayer of thanks for Tom Builder.

Tom saw him and came down off the pile. Before speaking to Philip he addressed one of the servants, the tailor who sewed the monks' clothes. "Start the monks carrying stones," he instructed the man. "Make sure they take only the stones I've marked, otherwise the pile may slip and kill someone." He turned to Philip. "I've marked enough to keep them going for a while."

"Where are they taking the stones?" Philip asked.

"Come and I'll show you. I want to check that they're stacking them properly."

Philip went with Tom. The stones were being taken to the east side of the priory close. "Some of the servants will still have to do their normal duties," Philip said as they walked. "The stable hands must still care for the horses, the cooks have to prepare meals, someone must fetch firewood and feed the chickens and go to market. But they're none of them overworked, and I can spare half of them. In addition, you'll have about thirty monks."

H e made a mat of woven reeds and pliable twigs, about three feet by two. He made neat wooden sides to the mat so that it had raised edges, like a tray. Then he burned some chalk for lime, mixed up a small quantity of strong plaster, and filled the tray with the mixture. As the mortar began to harden, he drew lines in it with a needle. He used his iron foot rule for straight lines, his set square for right angles and his compasses for curves.

He would do three drawings: a section, to explain how the church was constructed; an elevation, to illustrate its beautiful proportions; and a floor plan to show the accommodation. He began with the section.

He imagined that the cathedral was like a long loaf of bread, then he cut off the crust at the west end, to see inside, and he began to draw.

It was very simple. He drew a tall flat-topped archway. That was the nave, seen from the end. It would have a flat wooden ceiling, like the old church. Tom would have greatly preferred to build a curved stone vault, but he knew Philip could not afford it.

On top of the nave he drew a triangular roof. The width of the building was determined by the width of the roof, and that in turn was limited by the timber available. It was difficult to get hold of beams longer than about thirty-five feet—and they were fiercely expensive. (Good timber was so valuable that a fine tree was liable to be chopped down and sold by its owner long before it was that high.) The nave of Tom's cathedral would probably be thirty-two feet wide, or twice the length of Tom's iron pole.

The nave he had drawn was high, impossibly high. But a cathedral had to be a dramatic building, awe-inspiring in its size, pulling the eye heavenward with its loftiness. One reason people came to them was that cathedrals were the largest buildings in the world: a man who never went to a cathedral could go through life without seeing a building much bigger than the hovel he lived in.

Unfortunately, the building Tom had drawn would fall down. The weight of lead and timber in the roof would be too much for the walls, which would buckle outward and collapse. They had to be propped up.

For that purpose Tom drew two round-topped archways, half the height of the nave, one on either side. These were the aisles. They would have curved stone ceilings: since the aisles were lower and narrower, the expense of stone vaults was not so great. Each aisle would have a sloping lean-to roof.

The side aisles, joined to the nave by their stone vaults, provided some support, but they did not reach quite high enough. Tom would build extra supports, at intervals, in the roof space of the side aisles, above the vaulted ceiling and below the lean-to roof. · He drew one of them, a stone arch rising from the top of the aisle wall across to the nave wall. Where the support rested on the aisle wall, Tom braced it further with a massive buttress jutting out from the side of the church. He put a turret on top of the buttress, to add weight and make it look nicer.

You could not have an awesomely tall church without the strengthening elements of aisles, supports and buttresses; but this might be difficult to explain to a monk, and Tom had drawn the sketch to help make it clear.

He also drew the foundations, going far underground beneath the walls. Laymen were always surprised at how deep foundations were.

It was a simple drawing, too simple to be of much use to builders; but it should be right for showing to Prior Philip. Tom wanted him to understand what was being proposed, to visualize the building, and get excited about it.

It was hard to imagine a big, solid church when what was in front of you was a few lines, scratched in plaster. Philip would need all the help Tom could give him.

The walls he had drawn looked solid, seen end on, but they would not be. Tom now began to draw the side view of the nave wall, as seen from inside the church. It was pierced at three levels. The bottom half was hardly a wall at all: it was just a row of columns, their tops joined by semicircular arches. It was called the arcade. Through the archways of the arcade could be seen the round-headed windows of the aisles. The windows would be neatly lined up with the archways, so that light from outside could fall, unobstructed, into the nave. The columns in between would be lined up with the buttresses on the outside walls.

Above each arch of the arcade was a row of three small arches, forming the tribune gallery. No light would come through these, for behind them was the lean-to roof of the side aisle.

Above the gallery was the clerestory, so called because it was pierced with windows which lit the upper half of the nave.

In the days when the old Kingsbridge Cathedral had been built, masons had relied on thick walls for strength, and had nervously inserted mean little windows that let in hardly any light. Modern builders understood that a building would be strong enough if its walls were straight and true.

Tom designed the three levels of the nave wall—arcade, gallery and clerestory—strictly in the proportions 3:1:2. The arcade was half the height of the wall, and the gallery was one third of the rest. Proportion was everything in a church: it gave a subliminal feeling of rightness to the whole building. Studying the finished drawing, Tom thought it looked perfectly graceful. But would Philip think so? Tom could see the tiers of arches marching down the length of the church, with their moldings and carvings picked out by an afternoon sun . . . but would Philip see the same?

He began his third drawing. This was a floor plan of the church. In his imagination he

saw twelve arches in the arcade. The church was therefore divided into twelve sections, called bays. The nave would be six bays long, the chancel four. In between, taking up the space of the seventh and eighth bays, would be the crossing, with the transepts sticking out either side and the tower rising above.

All cathedrals and nearly all churches were cross-shaped. The cross was the single most important symbol of Christianity, of course, but there was a practical reason too: the transepts provided useful space for extra chapels and offices such as the sacristry and the vestry.

When he had drawn a simple floor plan Tom returned to the central drawing, which showed the interior of the church viewed from the west end. Now he drew the tower rising above and behind the nave.

The tower should be either one and a half times the height of the nave, or double it. The lower alternative gave the building an attractively regular profile, with the aisles, the nave and the tower rising in equal steps, 1:2:3. The higher tower would be more dramatic, for then the nave would be double the size of the aisles, and the tower double the nave, the proportions being 1:2:4. Tom had chosen the dramatic: this was the only cathedral he would ever build, and he wanted it to reach for the sky. He hoped Philip would feel the same.

If Philip accepted the design, Tom would have to draw it again, of course, more carefully and exactly to scale. And there would be many more drawings, hundreds of them: plinths, columns, capitals, corbels, doorcases, turrets, stairs, gargoyles, and countless other details—Tom would be drawing for years. But what he had in front of him was the essence of the building, and it was good: simple, inexpensive, graceful and perfectly proportioned.

He looked shrewdly at Tom. "Have you ever built a cathedral before?"

"No, though I've designed and built smaller churches. But I worked on Exeter Cathedral, for several years, finishing up as deputy master builder."

Tom hesitated. It was as well to be candid with Philip: the man had no patience for prevarication. "Yes, Father. I want you to appoint me master builder," he said as calmly as he could.

"Why?"

Tom had expected that question. There were so many reasons. *Because I've seen it done badly, and I know I could do it well,* he thought. *Because there is nothing more satisfying, to a master craftsman, than to exercise his skill, except perhaps to make love to a beautiful woman. Because something like this gives meaning to a man's life* . Which answer did Philip want? The prior would probably like him to say something pious. Recklessly, he decided to tell the real truth. "Because it will be beautiful," he said.

om had found a forester and a master quarryman in Salisbury, where Bishop Roger's palace was almost complete. The forester and his men had now been at work for two weeks, finding and felling tall pine trees and mature oaks. They were concentrating their efforts on the woods near the river, upstream from Kingsbridge, for it was very costly to transport materials on the winding mud roads, and a lot of money could be saved by simply floating the wood downstream to the building site. The timber would be roughly lopped for scaffolding poles, carefully shaped into templates to guide the masons and stonecarvers, or—in the case of the tallest trees—set aside for future use as roof beams. Good wood was now arriving in Kingsbridge at a steady rate and all Tom had to do was pay the foresters every Saturday evening.

The quarrymen had arrived over the last few days. The master quarryman, Otto Blackface, had brought with him his two sons, both of whom were stonecutters; four grandsons, all apprentices; and two laborers, one his cousin and the other his brother-in-law. Such nepotism was normal, and Tom had no objection to it: a family group usually made a good team.

As yet there were no craftsmen working in Kingsbridge, on the site itself, other than Tom and the priory's carpenter. It was a good idea to stockpile some materials. But soon Tom would hire the people who formed the backbone of the building team, the masons. They were the men who put one stone on another and made the walls rise. Then the great enterprise would begin. Tom walked with a spring in his step: this was what he had hoped for and worked toward for ten years.

Meanwhile, all his intellectual energy was employed in planning the cathedral. Otto and his team of stonecutters would build a rough lodge for themselves at the quarry, where they could sleep at night. When they were settled in, they would build real houses, and those who were married would bring their families to live with them.

Of all the building crafts, quarrying required the least skill and the most muscle. The master quarryman did the brainwork: he decided which zones would be mined and in what order; he arranged for ladders and lifting gear; if a sheer face was to be worked he would design scaffolding; he made sure there was a constant supply of tools coming from the smithy. Actually digging out the stones was relatively simple. The quarryman would use an iron-headed pickax to make an initial groove in the rock, then deepen it with a hammer and chisel. When the groove was big enough to weaken the rock, he would drive a wooden wedge into it. If he had judged his rock rightly, it would split exactly where he wanted.

Laborers removed the stones from the quarry, either carrying them on stretchers or lifting them with a rope attached to a huge winding wheel. In the lodge, stonecutters with axes would hack the stones roughly into the shape specified by the master builder.

Accurate carving and shaping would be done at Kingsbridge, of course.

The biggest problem would be transport. The quarry was a day's journey from the building site, and a carter would probably charge fourpence a trip—and he could not carry more than eight or nine of the big stones without breaking his cart or killing his horse. As soon as the quarrymen were settled in, Tom had to explore the area and see whether there were any waterways that could be used to shorten the journey.

❖

The new church would be bigger than the old one, but it would still be small for a cathedral. A part of Philip wanted it to be the longest, highest, richest and most beautiful cathedral in the kingdom, but he suppressed the wish, and told himself to be grateful for any kind of church.

He went into Tom's shed and looked at the woodwork on the bench. The builder had spent most of the winter in here, working with an iron measuring stick and a set of fine chisels, making what he called templates—wooden models for the masons to use as guides when they were cutting stones into shape. Philip had watched with admiration while Tom, a big man with big hands,

precisely and painstakingly carved the wood into perfect curves and square corners and exact angles. Now Philip picked up one of the templates and examined it. It was shaped like the edge of a daisy, a quarter-circle with several round projections like petals. What sort of stone needed to be that shape? He found that these things were hard to visualize, and he was constantly impressed by the power of Tom's imagination. He looked at Tom's drawings, engraved on plaster in wooden frames, and eventually he decided that he was holding a template for the piers of the arcade, which would look like clusters of shafts. Philip had thought they would actually be clusters of shafts, but now he realized that would be an illusion: the piers would be solid stone columns with shaft-like decorations.

Five years, Tom had said, and the east end would be finished. Five years, and Philip would be able to hold services in a cathedral again. All he had to do was find the money. This year it had been hard to scrape together enough cash to make a modest start, because his reforms were slow to take effect; but next year, after he had sold the new spring's wool, he would be able to hire more craftsmen and begin to build in earnest.

The first thing Tom did, when the laborers brought him a stone, was to take out an iron instrument shaped like the letter L and use it to check that the edges of the stone were square. Then he would shovel a layer of mortar on to the wall, furrow the mortar with the point of his trowel, put the new stone on, and scrape off the surplus mortar. In placing the stone he was guided by a taut string which was stretched between the two buttresses.

Philip noticed that the stone was almost as smooth on the top and bottom, where the mortar was, as on the side that would show. This surprised him, and he asked Tom the reason. "A stone must never touch the ones above or below," Tom replied. "That's what the mortar's for."

"Why must they not touch?"

"It causes cracks." Tom stood upright to explain. "If you tread on a slate roof, your foot will go through it; but if you put a plank across the roof, you can walk on it without damaging the slates. The plank spreads the weight, and that's what mortar does."

Philip had never thought of that. Building was an intriguing business, especially with someone like Tom, who was able to explain what he was doing.

The roughest face of the stone was the back. Surely, Philip thought, that face would be visible from inside the church? Then he recalled that Tom was in fact building a double-skinned wall with a cavity between, so that the back of each stone would be hidden.

When Tom had laid the stone on the bed of mortar, he picked up his level. This was an iron triangle with a leather thong attached to its apex and some markings on its base. The thong had a lead weight attached to it so that it always hung straight down. He put the base of the instrument on the stone and watched how the leather thong fell. If it hung to one side or the other of the center line, he would tap the stone with his hammer

until it was exactly level. Then he would move the instrument until it straddled the join between the two adjacent stones, to check that the tops of the stones were exactly in line. Finally he turned the instrument sideways on the stone to make sure it was not leaning one way or the other. Before picking up a new stone he would snap the taut string to satisfy himself that the faces of the stones were in a straight line. Philip had not realized it was so important that stone walls should be precisely straight and true.

He lifted his gaze to the rest of the building site. It was so big that eighty men and women and a few children were lost in it. They were working away cheerfully in the sunshine, but they were so few that it seemed to him there was an air of futility about their efforts. He had originally hoped for a hundred people, but now he saw that even that would not have been enough.

"Certainly." Tom returned to his wall, with the bishop's party in tow. He knelt over his mortarboard and spread the mortar in a uniform layer, smoothing the surface. Then, with the point of his trowel, he drew a sketch of the west end of the church in the mortar. He knew he was good at this. The bishop, his party, and all the monks and volunteer workers nearby watched in fascination. Drawing always seemed a miracle to people who could not do it. In a few moments Tom had created a line drawing of the west facade, with its three arched doorways, its big window, and its flanking turrets. It was a simple trick, but it never failed to impress.

"Remarkable," said Bishop Henry when the drawing was done. "May God's blessing be added to your skill."

Tom smiled. That amounted to a powerful endorsement of his appointment.

He kicked his horse forward and rode across the graveyard to the building site, curious to see it more closely.

The eight massive piers of the arcade marched down either side of the site in four opposed pairs. From a distance, William had thought he could see the round arches joining one pier with the next, but now he realized the arches were not built yet—what he had seen was the wooden falsework, made in the same shape, upon which the stones would rest while the arches were being constructed and the mortar was drying. The falsework did not rest on the ground, but was supported on the out-jutting moldings of the capitals on top of the piers.

Parallel with the arcade, the outer walls of the aisles were going up, with regular spaces for the windows. Midway between each window opening, a buttress jutted out from the line of the wall. Looking at the open ends of the unfinished walls, William could see that they were not solid stone: they were in fact double walls with a space in between. The cavity appeared to be filled with rubble and mortar.

The scaffolding was made of stout poles roped together, with trestles of flexible saplings and woven reeds laid across the poles.

A lot of money had been spent here, William noted.

❖

To Philip's right, no more than a quarter of a mile from the castle gate, was the west front of the cathedral, and Philip saw instantly that despite its proximity to the castle it had been taken over as the king's military headquarters. A line of sentries barred the narrow road that led between the canons' houses to the church. Beyond the sentries, knights and men-at-arms were passing in and out through the three doorways to the cathedral. The graveyard was an army camp, with tents and cooking fires and horses grazing the turf. There were no monastic buildings: Lincoln Cathedral was not run by monks, but by priests called canons, who lived in ordinary town houses near the church.

The space between the cathedral and the castle was empty except for Philip and his companions. Philip suddenly realized that they had the full attention of the guards on the king's side and the sentries on the opposing ramparts. He was in the no-man's-land between the two armed camps, probably the most dangerous spot in Lincoln. Looking around, he saw that Richard and the others had already moved on, and he followed them hastily.

The king's sentries let them through immediately: Richard was well known. Philip admired the west facade of the cathedral. It had an enormously tall entrance arch, and subsidiary arches on either side, half the size of the central one but still awesome. It looked like the gateway to heaven—which it was, of course, in a way. Philip immediately

decided he wanted tall arches in the west front of Kingsbridge Cathedral.

Leaving the horses with the squire, Philip and Richard made their way through the encampment and entered the cathedral. It was even more crowded inside than out. The aisles had been turned into stables, and hundreds of horses were tied to the columns of the arcade. Armed men thronged the nave, and here too there were cooking fires and bedding. Some spoke English, some French, and a few spoke Flemish, the guttural tongue of the wool merchants of Flanders. By and large the knights were in here and the men-at-arms were outside. Philip was sorry to see several men playing at ninemen's morris for money, and he was even more disturbed by the appearance of some of the women, who were dressed very skimpily for winter and appeared to be flirting with the men—almost, he thought, as if they were sinful women, or even, God forbid, whores.

To avoid looking at them he raised his eyes to the ceiling. It was of wood, and beautifully painted in glowing colors, but it was a terrible fire risk with all those people cooking in the nave. He followed Richard through the crowd. Richard seemed at ease here, assured and confident, calling out greetings to barons and lords, and slapping knights on the back.

The crossing and the east end of the cathedral had been roped off. The east end appeared to have been reserved for the priests—I should think so, too, Philip thought—and the crossing had become the king's quarters.

Work stopped at noon on Saint Augustine's Day. Most of the builders greeted the midday bell with a sigh of relief. They normally worked from sunrise to sunset, six days a week, so they needed the rest they got on holy days. However, Jack was too absorbed in his work to hear the bell.

He was mesmerized by the challenge of making soft, round shapes out of hard rock. The stone had a wall of its own, and if he tried to make it do something it did not want to do, it would fight him, and his chisel would slip, or dig in too deeply, spoiling the shapes. But once he had got to know the lump of rock in front of him he could transform it. The more difficult the task, the more fascinated he was. He was beginning to feel that the decorative carving demanded by Tom was too easy. Zigzags, lozenges, dogtooth, spirals and plain roll moldings bored him, and even these leaves were rather stiff and repetitive. He wanted to carve natural-looking foliage, pliable and irregular, and copy the different shapes of real leaves, oak and ash and birch, but Tom would not let him. Most of all he wanted to carve scenes from stories, Adam and Eve, David and Goliath, and the Day of Judgment, with monsters and devils and naked people, but he did not dare to ask.

Eventually Tom made him stop work. "It's a holiday, lad," he said. "Besides, you're still my apprentice, and I want you to help me clear up. All tools must be locked away before dinner."

Jack put away his hammer and chisels, and carefully deposited the stone on which he had been working in Tom's shed; then he went around the site with Tom. The other apprentices were tidying up and sweeping away the stone chips, sand, lumps of dried mortar and wood shavings that littered the site. Tom picked up his compasses and level while Jack collected his yardsticks and plumb lines, and they took everything to the shed.

"But what's the point of having everything measured . . . ? Why not build it all higgedly-piggedly, like a house?"

"First, because it's cheaper this way. All the arches of the arcade are identical, so we can reuse the falsework arches. The fewer different sizes and shapes of stone we need, the fewer templates I have to make. And so on. Second, it simplifies every aspect of what we're doing, from the original laying-out—everything is based on a pole square—to painting the walls—it's easier to estimate how much whitewash we'll need. And when things are simple, fewer mistakes are made. The most expensive part of a building is the mistakes. Third, when everything is based on a pole measure, the church just looks right. Proportion is the heart of beauty."

Jack nodded, enchanted. The struggle to control an operation as ambitious and intricate as building a cathedral was endlessly fascinating. The notion that the principles of regularity and repetition could both simplify the construction and result in a harmonious building was a seductive idea. But he was not sure whether proportion was the heart of beauty. He had a taste for wild, spreading, disorderly things: high mountains, aged oaks, and Aliena's hair.

Work on the new cathedral had slowed dramatically, as it always did a month or so before Christmas. The exposed edges and tops of the unfinished stonework were covered with straw and dung—the litter from the prior stables—to keep the frost off the new masonry. The mason could not build in the winter, because of the frost, they said. Philip had asked why they could not uncover the walls every morning and cover them again at night: it was not often frosty in the daytime. Tom said that walls built in winter fell down. Philip believed that, but he did not think it was because of the frost. He thought the real reason might be that the mortar took several months to set properly. The winter break allowed it to get really hard before the new year's masonry was built on top. That would also explain the masons' superstition that it was bad luck to build more than twenty feet high in a single year: more than that, and the lower courses might become deformed by the weight on them before the mortar could harden.

Philip was surprised to see all the masons out in the open, in what would be the chancel of the church. He went to see what they were doing.

They had made a semicircular wooden arch and stood it upright, propped up with poles on both sides. Philip knew that the wooden arch was a piece of what they called falsework: its purpose was to support the stone arch while it was being built. Now, however, the masons were assembling the stone arch at ground level, without mortar, to make sure the stones fit together perfectly. Apprentices and laborers were lifting the stones onto the falsework while the masons looked on critically.

Philip caught Tom's eye and said: "What's this for?"

"It's an arch for the tribune gallery."

Philip looked up reflexively. The arcade had been finished last year and the gallery above it would be completed next year. Then only the top level, the clerestory, would remain to be built before the roof went on. Now that the walls had been covered up for the winter, the masons were cutting the stones ready for next year's work. If this arch was right, the stones for all the others would be cut to the same patterns.

The apprentices, among whom was Tom's stepson, Jack, built the arch up from either side, with the wedge-shaped stones called voussoirs. Although the arch would eventually be built high up in the church, it would have elaborate decorative moldings; so each stone bore, on the surface that would be visible, a line of large dogtooth carving, another line of small medallions, and a bottom line of simple roll molding. When the stones were put together, the carvings lined up exactly, forming three continuous arcs, one of dogtooth, one of medallions and one of roll molding. This gave the impression that the arch was constructed of several semicircular hoops of stone one on top of another, whereas, in fact, it was made of wedges

placed side by side. However, the stones had to fit together precisely, otherwise the carvings would not line up and the illusion would be spoiled.

Philip watched while Jack lowered the central keystone into place. Now the arch was complete. Four masons picked up sledgehammers and knocked out the wedges that supported the wooden falsework a few inches above the ground. Dramatically, the wooden support fell. Although there was no mortar between the stones, the arch remained standing. Tom Builder gave a grunt of satisfaction.

❖

He was mean to his stepsister, Martha, who was almost as hurt by him as he was by Aliena. On Sunday afternoons he wasted his wages gambling on cockfights. All his passion came out in his work. He was carving corbels, the jutting-out stones that appeared to support arches or shafts that did not reach all the way to the ground. Corbels were often decorated with leaves, but a traditional alternative was to carve a man who appeared to be holding up the arch with his hands or supporting it on his back. Jack altered the customary pattern just a little, but the effect was to show a disturbingly twisted human figure with an expression of pain, condemned, as it were, to an eternity of agony as he held up the vast weight of stone. Jack knew it was brilliant: nobody else could carve a figure that looked as if it were in pain. When Tom saw it he shook his head, unsure whether to marvel at its expressiveness or disapprove of its unorthodoxy. Philip was very taken with it. Jack did not care what they thought: he felt that anyone who disliked it was blind.

❖

Nevertheless, he was contemplating taking the vows. He did not have to keep them. All he cared about was building the cathedral. The problems of supply, construction and management were endlessly absorbing. One day he might have to help Tom devise a method of checking that the number of stones arriving at the site was the same as the number leaving the quarry—a complex problem, for the journey time varied between two days and four, so it was not possible to have a simple daily tally. Another day the masons might complain that the carpenters were not making the falsework properly. Most challenging of all were the engineering problems, such as how to lift tons of stone to the top of the walls using makeshift machinery fixed to flimsy scaffolding. Tom Builder discussed these problems with Jack as with an equal. He seemed to have forgiven Jack for that angry speech, in which Jack said that Tom had never done anything for him. And Tom acted as if he had forgotten the revelation that Jack had set fire to the old cathedral. They worked together cheerfully, and the days flew by. Even during the tedious services Jack's mind was occupied by some knotty question of construction or planning. His knowledge was increasing fast. Instead of spending years carving stones, he was learning cathedral design. There could hardly have been a better training for someone who wanted to be a master builder. For that, Jack was prepared to yawn through any number of midnight matins.

❖

Building Kingsbridge Cathedral was the most profoundly satisfying work he had ever done. He was responsible for the design and the execution. No one interfered with him, and there was no one else to blame if things went wrong. As the mighty walls rose, with their rhythmic arches, their graceful moldings, and their individual carvings, he could look around and think: I did all this, and I did it well.

❖

He felt a moment of panic. He wanted to yell *Don't move, you'll fall!* but his words would have been lost in the noise of the fair. He pushed through the crowd toward the cathedral. Jonathan was running along the scaffolding, absorbed in some imaginary game, heedless of the danger that he might slip and fall over the edge and tumble eighty feet to his death—

Tom quenched the terror rising like bile in his throat.

The scaffolding did not rest on the ground,

but on heavy timber inserted into purpose-built holes high up in the walls. These timbers jutted out six feet or so. Stout poles were laid across them and roped to them, and then trestles made of flexible saplings and woven reeds were laid on the poles. The scaffolding was normally reached via the spiral stone staircases built into the thickness of the walls. But those staircases had been closed off today. So how had Jonathan climbed up? There were no ladders—Tom had seen to that, and Jack had double-checked. The child must have climbed up the stepped end of the unfinished wall. The ends had been built up with wood, so that they no longer provided easy access; but Jonathan could have clambered over the blocks. The child was full of self-confidence—but all the same he fell over at least once a day.

Tom reached the foot of the wall and looked up fearfully. Jonathan was playing happily eighty feet above. Fear gripped Tom's heart with a cold hand. He shouted at the top of his voice: "Jonathan!"

Tom realized he was going to have to go up and get him. "Just stay where you are until I reach you!" he shouted. He pushed the blocks of wood off the lower steps and mounted the wall.

It was four feet wide at the foot, but it narrowed as it went up. Tom climbed steadily. He was tempted to rush, but he forced himself to be calm. When he glanced up he saw Jonathan sitting on the edge of the scaffolding, dangling his short legs over the sheer drop.

At the very top the wall was only two feet thick. Even so, it was plenty wide enough to walk on, provided you had strong nerves, and Tom did. He made his way along the wall, jumped down onto the scaffolding, and took Jonathan in his arms. He was swamped with relief. "You foolish boy," he said, but his voice was full of love, and Jonathan hugged him.

❖

P hilip was in the undercroft beneath the priory kitchen, counting money with Cuthbert Whitehead, when he heard the noise. He and Cuthbert looked at one another, frowning, then got up to see what was going on.

They stepped through the door into a riot.

Philip was horrified. People were running in every direction, pushing and shoving, falling over and treading on one another. Men and women were shouting, and children were crying. The air was full of smoke. Everyone seemed to be trying to get out of the priory close. Apart from the main gate, the only exit was through the gap between the kitchen buildings and the mill. There was no wall there, but there was a deep ditch that carried water from the millpond to the brewery. Philip wanted to warn people to be careful of the ditch, but nobody was listening to anyone.

The cause of the rush was obviously a fire, and a very big one. The air was thick with the smoke of it. Philip was full of fear. With this many people all crowded together, the slaughter could be appalling. What could be done? . . . How could this be happening? . . .

He saw a large blond man on a massive war-horse crashing through the crowds of people. It was William Hamleigh. . . .

Philip yelled: "You'll go to hell for this!"

William's face was suffused with bloodlust. Even the threat of what he feared most had no effect on him today. He was like a madman. He waved his firebrand in the air like a banner. "This is hell, monk!" he shouted back; and he wheeled his horse and rode on.

The storehouse was an inferno, and smaller fires burned all around. The ground was littered with bodies, some moving, some bleeding, some limp and still. Apart from the crackle of flames it was quiet. The mob had got out, one way or another, leaving their dead and wounded behind. Jack felt dazed. He had never seen a battlefield but he imagined it must look like this.

His stepfather's tall body was stretched out full length on the muddy ground. It was perfectly still. His face was recognizable, even peaceful-looking, up to the eyebrows; but his forehead was open and his skull was completely smashed. Jack was appalled. He could not take it in. Tom could not be dead. But this thing could not be alive. He looked away, then he looked back. It was Tom, and he was dead.

Jack knelt beside the body. He felt the urge to do something, or say something, and for the first time he understood why people liked to pray for the dead. "Mother is going to miss you terribly," he said. He remembered the angry speech he had made to Tom on the day of his fight with Alfred. "Most of that wasn't true," he said, and the tears started to flow. "You didn't fail me. You fed me and took care of me, and you made my mother happy, truly happy." But there was something more important than that, he thought. What Tom had given him was nothing so commonplace as food and shelter. Tom had given him something unique, something no other man had to give, something even his own father could not have given him; something that was a passion, a skill, an art, and a way of life. "You gave me the cathedral," Jack whispered to the dead man. "Thank you."

She walked along the southern side aisle, dragging her hand along the wall, feeling the rough texture of the stones, running her fingernails over the shallow grooves made by the stonemason's tooth chisel. Here in the aisles, under the windows, the wall was decorated with blind arcading, like a row of filled-in arches. The arcading served no purpose but it added to the sense of harmony Aliena felt when she looked at the building. Everything in Tom's cathedral looked as if it was meant to be. Perhaps her life was like that, everything foreordained in a grand design, and she was like a foolish builder who wanted a waterfall in the chancel.

In the southeast corner of the church, a low doorway led to a narrow spiral staircase. On impulse Aliena went through the doorway and climbed the stairs. When she lost sight of the doorway, and could not yet see the top of the stairs, she began to feel peculiar, for the passage looked as if it might wind upward forever. Then she saw daylight: there was a small slit window in the turret wall, put there to light the steps. Eventually she emerged onto the wide gallery over the aisle. It had no windows to the outside, but on the inside it looked into the roofless church. She sat on the sill of one of the inner arches, leaning against the pillar. The cold stone caressed her cheek. She wondered whether Jack had carved this one. It occurred to her that if she fell from here she might die. But it was not really high enough: she might just break her legs, and lie in agony until the monks came and found her.

She decided to climb to the clerestory.

She returned to the turret staircase and went on up. The next stage was shorter, but still she found it frightening, and her heart was beating loudly by the time she reached the top. She stepped into the clerestory passage, a narrow tunnel in the wall. She edged along the passage until it came out onto the inner sill of a clerestory window. She held on to the pillar that divided the window. When she looked down at the seventy-five-foot drop, she started to shake.

She heard footsteps on the turret stairs. She found herself breathing hard, as if she had been running. There had been no one else in sight. Had someone crept up behind her, trying to sneak up on her? The steps came along the clerestory passage. She let go of the pillar and stood teetering on the edge. A figure appeared on the sill. It was Jack. Her heart beat so loudly she could hear it.

T he rumbling was at first mystifying. For a moment or two he thought it was thunder; then it grew too loud, and the people stopped singing. Still Philip thought it was only some strange phenomenon, shortly to be explained, whose worst effect would be to interrupt the service. Then he looked up.

In the third bay, where the falsework had come down only this morning, cracks were appearing in the masonry, high on the walls, at the clerestory level. They appeared suddenly and flashed across the wall from one clerestory window to the next like striking snakes. Philip's first reaction was disappointment: he had been happy that the chancel was finished, but now he would have to undertake repairs, and all the people who had been so impressed with the builders'

work would say: "More haste, less speed." Then the tops of the walls seemed to lean outward, and he realized with an awful sense of horror that this was not merely going to interrupt the service, this was going to be a catastrophe.

Cracks appeared in the curved vault. A big stone became detached from the web of the masonry and tumbled slowly through the air. People started screaming and trying to get out of its way. Before Philip could see

whether anyone was badly hurt, more stone began to fall. The congregation panicked, pushing and shoving and trampling on one another as they tried to dodge the falling stones. Philip had the wild thought that this was another attack of some kind by William Hamleigh; then he saw William, at the front of the congregation, battering people around him in a terrified bid to escape, and realized that William would not have done this to himself.

Most people were trying to move away from the altar, to get out of the cathedral through the open west end. But it was the westernmost part of the building, the open end, that was collapsing. The problem was in the third bay. In the second bay, where Philip was, the vault seemed to be holding; and behind him, in the first bay where the monks were lined up, it looked solid. At that end the opposite walls were held together by the east facade.

He saw little Jonathan, with Johnny Eightpence, both huddled at the far end of the north aisle. They were safer there than anywhere, Philip decided; and then he realized that he should try and get the rest of his flock to safety. "Come this way!" he shouted. "Everybody! Move this way!" Whether they heard him or not, they took no notice.

In the third bay, the tops of the walls crumbled, falling outward, and the entire vault collapsed, large and small stones falling through the air like a lethal hailstorm to land on the hysterical congregation. Philip darted forward and grabbed a citizen. "Go back!" he yelled, and shoved the man toward the east end. The startled man saw the monks huddled against the far wall and dashed to join them. Philip did the same to two women. The people with them realized what he was doing and moved east without being pushed. Other people began to get the idea, and a general move east began among those who had been at the front of the congregation.

Looking up for an instant, Philip was appalled to see that the second bay was going to go: the same cracks were snaking across the clerestory and frosting the vault directly over his head. He continued to herd people to the safety of the east end, knowing that every person he moved might be a life saved. A rain of crumbled mortar fell on his shaved head, and then the stones started to come down. The people were scattering. Some had taken refuge in the shelter of the side aisles; some were crowded up against the east wall, among them Bishop Waleran; others were still trying to crowd out of the west end, crawling over the fallen rubble and

bodies in the third bay. A stone hit Philip's shoulder. It was a glancing blow but it hurt. He put his hands over his head and looked around wildly. He was alone in the middle of the second bay: everyone else was around the edges of the danger zone. He had done all he could. He ran to the east end.

There he turned again and looked up. The clerestory of the second bay was collapsing now, and the vault was falling into the chancel, in exact replication of what had happened in the third bay; but there were fewer victims, because the people had had a chance to get out of the way, and because the roofs of the side aisles appeared to be holding there, whereas in the third bay they had given way. Everyone in the crowd at the east end moved back, pressing up against the wall, and all faces were turned up, watching the vault, to see whether the collapse would spread to the first bay. The crash of falling masonry seemed to become less loud, but a fog of dust and small stones filled the air and for a few moments no one could see anything. Philip held his breath. The dust cleared and he could see the vault again. It had collapsed right up to the edge of the first bay; but now it seemed to be holding.

The dust settled. Everything went quiet. Philip stared aghast at the ruins of his church. Only the first bay remained intact. The walls of the second bay were standing up to the level of the gallery, but in the third and fourth bays only the side aisles were left, and they were badly damaged. The floor of the church was a pile of rubble littered with the still or feebly moving bodies of the dead and injured. Seven years of work and hundreds of pounds in money had been destroyed, and dozens of people had been killed, maybe hundreds, all in a few terrible moments. Philip's heart ached for the wasted work and the lost people, and for the widows and orphans left behind; and his eyes filled with bitter tears.

Jack smiled. "When I left Kingsbridge, riding my mother's horse, with my stepfather's tools in a satchel slung across my shoulder, I thought there was only one way to build a church: thick walls with round arches and small windows topped by a wooden ceiling or a barrel-shaped stone vault. The cathedrals I saw on my way from Kingsbridge to Southampton taught me no different. But Normandy changed my life."

"I can imagine," Raschid said sleepily. He was not very interested, so Jack recalled those days in silence. Within hours of landing at Honfleur he was looking at the abbey church of Jumieges. It was the highest church he had ever seen, but otherwise it had the usual round arches and wooden ceiling—

except in the chapter house, where Abbot Urso had built a revolutionary stone ceiling. Instead of a smooth, continuous barrel, or a creased groin vault, this ceiling had ribs which sprang up from the tops of the columns and met at the apex of the roof. The ribs were thick and strong, and the triangular sections of ceiling between the ribs were thin and light. The monk who was keeper of the fabric explained to Jack that it was easier to build that way: the ribs were put up first, and the sections between were then simpler to make. This type of vault was also lighter. The monk was hoping to hear news from Jack of technical innovations in England, and Jack had to disappoint him. However, Jack's evident appreciation of rib-vaulting pleased the

monk, and he told Jack that there was a church at Lessay, not far away, that had rib-vaulting throughout.

Jack went to Lessay the next day, and spent all afternoon in the church, staring in wonder at the vault. What was so striking about it, he finally decided, was the way the ribs, coming down from the apex of the vault to the capitals on top of the columns, seemed to *dramatize* the way the weight of the roof was being carried by the strongest members. The ribs made the logic of the building visible.

❖

Nevertheless, the journey was by no means wasted. Every arch Jack had ever seen, until the moment he entered the abbey church of Cluny, had been semicircular; and every vault had been either tunnel-shaped, like a long line of round arches all stuck together, or groined, like the crossing where two tunnels met. The arches at Cluny were not semicircular.

They rose to a point.

There were pointed arches in the main arcades; the groined vaults of the side aisles had pointed arches; and—most startling of all—above the nave there was a stone ceiling that could only be described as a pointed barrel vault. Jack had always been taught that a circle was strong because it was perfect,

and a round arch was strong because it was part of a circle. He would have thought that pointed arches were considerably stronger than the old round ones. The church at Cluny seemed to prove it, for despite the great weight of stonework in its peaked vault, it was very high.

Jack did not stay long at Cluny. He continued south, following the pilgrim road, diverging whenever the whim took him. In the early summer there were jongleurs all along the route, in the larger towns or near the Cluniac monasteries. They recited their verse narratives to crowds of pilgrims in front of churches and shrines, sometimes accompanying themselves on the viol, just the way Aliena had told him. Jack approached every

one and asked if he had known Jack Shareburg. They all said no.

The churches he saw on his way through southwest France and northern Spain continued to astonish him. They were all much higher than the English cathedrals. Some of them had banded barrel vaults. The bands, reaching from pier to pier across the vault of the church, made it possible to build in stages, bay by bay, instead of all at once. They also changed the look of a church. By emphasizing the divisions between bays, they revealed that the building was a series of identical units, like a sliced loaf; and this imposed order and logic on the huge interior space.

He could never work on another church like Kingsbridge Cathedral, he thought as he sat in the warm Spanish afternoon, listening vaguely to the laughter of the women somewhere deep in the big cool house. He still wanted to build the most beautiful cathedral in the world, but it would not be a massive, solid, fortress-like structure. He wanted to use the new techniques, the rib-vaults and the pointed arches. However, he thought he would not use them in quite the way they had been used so far. None of the churches he had seen had made the most of the possibilities. A picture of a church was forming in his mind. The details were hazy but the overall feeling was very strong: it was a spacious, airy building, with sunlight pouring through its huge windows, and an arched vault so high it seemed to reach heaven.

Jack entered the town and reined in his horse in the middle of the marketplace to look up at the west front of the church. There was nothing revolutionary here. It was a straightforward old-fashioned facade with twin towers and three round-arched doorways. He rather liked the aggressive way the piers thrust out from the wall, but he would not have ridden five miles to see that.

He tied his horse to a rail in front of the church and went closer. The sculpture around the three portals was quite good: lively subjects, precisely chiseled. Jack went in.

Inside there was an immediate change. Before the nave proper, there was a low entryway, or narthex. As Jack looked up at the ceiling he experienced a surge of excite-

ment. The builders had used rib-vaulting and pointed arches in combination here, and Jack saw in a flash that the two techniques went together perfectly: the grace of the pointed arch was accentuated by the ribs that followed its line.

There was more to it. In between the ribs, instead of the usual web of mortar-and-rubble, this builder had put cut stones, as in a wall. Being stronger, the layer of stones could probably be thinner, and therefore lighter, Jack realized.

As he stared up, craning his neck until it ached, he understood a further remarkable feature of this combination. Two pointed arches of different widths could be made to reach the same height, merely by adjusting the curve of the arch. This gave the bay a more regular look. It could not be done with round arches, of course: the height of a semicircular arch was always half its width, so a wide one had to be higher than a narrow one. That meant that in a rectangular bay, the narrow arches had to spring from a point higher up the wall than the springing of the wide ones, so that their tops would be at the same level and the ceiling would be even. The result was always lopsided. This problem had now vanished.

He walked along the south aisle to the crossing. As he got nearer to the chancel he sensed that something quite remarkable was ahead of him. There was, indeed, sunlight pouring in, but the vault appeared to be complete and there were no gaps in the walls. When Jack stepped out of the aisle into the crossing he saw that the sun was streaming in through rows of tall windows, some of them made of colored glass, and all this sunshine seemed to fill the vast empty vessel of the church with warmth and light. Jack could not understand how they had got so much window area: there seemed to be more window than wall. He was awestruck. How had this been done, if not by magic?

The principle of rib-vaulting was that a ceiling was made of a few strong ribs, with the gaps between the ribs filled in with light material. *They had applied that principle to the whole building.* The wall of the chancel consisted of a few strong piers joined by windows. The arcade separating the chancel from its side aisles was not a wall but a row of piers joined by pointed arches, leaving wide spaces through which the light from the windows could fall into the middle of the church. The aisle itself was divided in two by a row of thin columns.

Pointed arches and rib-vaulting had been combined here, as they had in the narthex, but it was now clear that the narthex had been a cautious trial for the new technology. By comparison with this, the narthex was musclebound, its ribs and moldings too heavy, its arches too small. Here everything was thin, light, delicate and airy. The simple roll moldings were all narrow and the colonettes were long and thin.

It would have looked too fragile to stay upright, except that the ribs showed so clearly how the weight of the building was being carried by the piers and columns. Here was a visible demonstration that a big building did not need thick walls with tiny windows and massive piers. Provided the weight was distributed precisely on a load-bearing skeleton, the rest of the building could be light stonework, glass, or empty space. Jack was spellbound. It was almost like falling in love. Euclid had been a revelation, but this was more than a revelation, for it was beautiful too. He had had visions of a church like this, and now he was actually looking at it, touching it, standing under its sky-high vault.

He walked around the curved east end in a daze, staring at the vaulting of the double aisle. The ribs arched over his head like branches in a forest of perfect stone trees. Here, as in the narthex, the filling between the ceiling ribs was cut stone jointed with mortar, instead of the easier, but heavier, rubble-and-mortar. The outer wall of the aisle had pairs of big windows with pointed tops to match the pointed arches. The revolutionary architecture was perfectly complemented by the colored windows. Jack had never seen colored glass in England, but he had come across several examples in France: however, in the small windows of an old-style church it could not achieve its full potential. Here, the effect of the morning sun pouring through the rich many-colored windows was more than beautiful, it was spellbinding.

Because the church was round-ended, the side aisles curved around to meet at the east end, forming a semicircular ambulatory or walkway. Jack walked all the way around the half circle, then turned and came back, still marveling. He returned to his starting point.

There he saw a woman.

He recognized her.

She smiled.

His heart stood still.

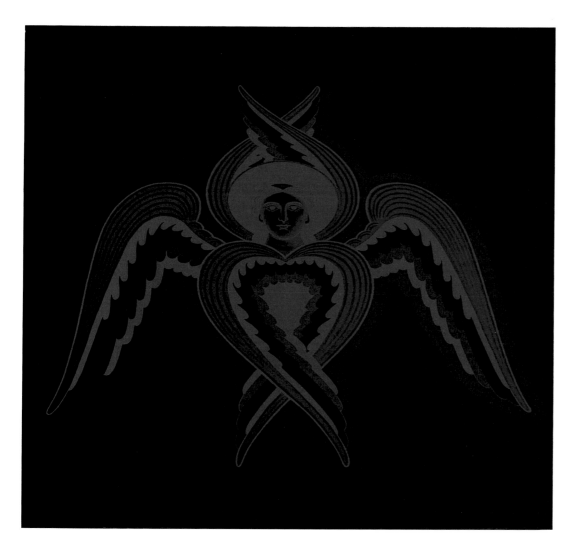

S ermons were becoming more common in churches. They had been rare when Philip was a boy. Abbot Peter had been against them, saying they tempted the priest to indulge himself. The old-fashioned view was that the congregation should be mere spectators, silently witnessing the mysterious holy rites, hearing the Latin words without understanding them, blindly trusting in the efficacy of the priest's intercession. But ideas had changed. Progressive thinkers nowadays no longer saw the congregation as mute observers of a mystical ceremony. The Church was supposed to be an integral part of their everyday existence. It marked the milestones in their lives, from christening, through marriage and the birth of children, to extreme unction and burial in consecrated ground. It might be their landlord, judge, employer or customer. Increasingly, people were expected to be Christians every day, not just on Sundays. They needed more than just rituals, according to the modern view: they wanted explanations, rulings, encouragement, exhortation.

After seven years Jack had finished the transepts—the two arms of the cross-shaped church—and they were everything he had hoped for. He had improved on the ideas of Saint-Denis, making everything taller and narrower—windows, arches, and the vault itself. The clustered shafts of the piers rose gracefully through the gallery and became the ribs of the vault, curving over to meet in the middle of the ceiling, and the tall pointed windows flooded the interior with light. The moldings were fine and delicate, and the carved decoration was a riot of stone foliage.

And there were cracks in the clerestory.

He stood in the high clerestory passage, staring out across the chasm of the north transept, brooding on a bright spring morning. He was shocked and baffled. By all the wisdom of the masons the structure was strong; but a crack showed a weakness. His vault was higher than any other he had ever seen, but not by that much. He had not made the mistake of Alfred, and put a stone vault on a structure that was not built to take the weight: his walls had been designed for a stone vault. Yet cracks had appeared in his clerestory in roughly the same place where Alfred's had failed. Alfred had miscalculated but Jack was sure he had not done the same thing. Some new factor was operating in Jack's building and he did not know what it was.

It was not dangerous, not in the short term. The cracks had been filled with mortar and they had not yet reappeared. The building was safe. But it was weak; and for Jack the weakness spoiled it. He wanted his church to last until the Day of Judgment.

He left the clerestory and went down the turret staircase to the gallery, where he had made his tracing floor, in the corner where there was a good light from one of the windows in the north porch. He began to draw

the plinth of a nave pier. He drew a diamond, then a square inside the diamond, then a circle inside the square. The main shafts of the pier would spring from the four points of the diamond and rise up the column, eventually branching off north, south, east and west to become arches or ribs. Subsidiary shafts, springing from the corners of the square, would rise to become vaulting ribs, going diagonally across the nave vault on

the other. The circle in the middle represented the core of the pier.

All Jack's designs were based on simple geometrical shapes and some not-so-simple proportions, such as the ratio of the square root of two to the square root of three. Jack had learned how to figure square roots in Toledo, but most masons could not calculate them, and instead used simple geometric constructions. They knew that if a circle was

drawn around the four corners of a square, the diameter of the circle was bigger than the side of the square in the ratio of the square root of two to one. That ratio, root-two to one, was the most ancient of the masons' formulas, for in a simple building it was the ratio of the outside width to the inside width, and therefore gave the thickness of the wall.

Jack's task was much complicated by the

religious significance of various numbers. Prior Philip was planning to rededicate the church to the Virgin Mary, because the Weeping Madonna worked more miracles than the tomb of Saint Adophus; and in consequence he wanted Jack to use the numbers nine and seven, which were Mary's numbers. He had designed the nave with nine bays and the new chancel, to be built when all else was finished, with seven. The interlocked blind arcading in the side aisles would have seven arches per bay, and the west facade would have nine lancet windows. Jack had no opinion about the theological significance of numbers but he felt instinctively that if the same numbers were used fairly consistently it was bound to add to the harmony of the finished building.

Before he could finish his drawing of the plinth he was interrupted by the master roofer, who had hit a problem and wanted Jack to solve it.

Jack followed the man up the turret staircase, past the clerestory, and into the roof space. They walked across the rounded domes that were the top side of the ribbed vault. Above them, the roofers were unrolling great sheets of lead and nailing them to the rafters, starting at the bottom and working up so that the upper sheets would overlap the lower and keep the rain out.

Jack saw the problem immediately. He had put a decorative pinnacle at the end of a valley between two sloping roofs, but he had left the design to a master mason, and the mason had not made provision for rainwater from the roof to pass through or under the pinnacle. The mason would have to alter it. He told the master roofer to pass this instruction on to the mason, then he returned to his tracing floor.

Ｈe looked up at the new transepts. His pleasure in his own creation was blighted by the cracks. They had reappeared on the day after the great storm. He was terribly disappointed. It had been a phenomenal tempest, of course, but his church was designed to survive a hundred such storms. He shook his head in perplexity, and climbed the turret stairs to the gallery. He wished he could talk to someone who had built a similar church, but nobody in England had, and even in France they had not yet gone this high.

On impulse, he did not go to his tracing floor, but continued up the staircase to the roof. The lead had all been laid and he saw that the pinnacle that had been blocking the flow of rainwater now had a generous gutter running through its base. It was windy up on the roof, and he tried to keep hold of something whenever he was near the edge: he would not be the first builder to be blown off a roof to his death by a gust of wind. The wind always seemed stronger up here than it did on the ground. In fact, the wind seemed to increase disproportionately as you climbed. . . .

He stood still, staring into space. That was the answer to his puzzle. It was not the *weight* of his vault that was causing the cracks—it was the *height*. He had built the church strong enough to bear the weight, he was sure; but he had not thought about the wind. These towering walls were constantly buffeted, and because they were so high, the wind was enough to crack them. Standing on the roof, feeling its force, he could just imagine the effect it was having on the tautly balanced structure below him. He knew the building so well that he could almost feel the strain, as if the walls were part of his body. The wind pushed sideways against the church, just as it was pushing against him; and because the church could not bend, it cracked.

He was quite sure he had found the explanation; but what was he going to do about it? He needed to strengthen the clerestory so that it could withstand the wind. But how? To build massive buttresses up against the walls would destroy the stunning effect of lightness and grace that he had achieved so successfully.

But if that was what it took to make the building stand up, he would have to do it.

❖

A huge iron ball hung by a chain from a wooden scaffold, like a hangman's noose dangling from a gallows. There was also a rope tied to the ball. This rope ran over a pulley on the upright post of the scaffold and hung down to the ground, where two laborers held it. When the laborers hauled on the rope, the ball was pulled up and back until it touched the pulley, and the chain lay horizontally along the arm of the scaffold.

Most of the population of Shiring was watching.

The men let go of the rope. The iron ball dropped and swung, smashing into the wall of the church. There was a terrific thud, the wall shuddered, and William felt the impact in the ground beneath his feet. He thought how he would like to have Richard clamped to the wall in just the place where the ball would hit. He would be squashed like a fly.

The laborers hauled on the rope again.

William realized he was holding his breath as the iron ball stopped at the top of its travel. The men let go; the ball swung; and this time it tore a hole in the stone wall. The crowd applauded.

It was an ingenious mechanism.

William was happy to see work progressing on the site where he would build the new church, but he had more urgent matters on his mind today. He looked around for Bishop Waleran, and spotted him standing with Alfred Builder. William approached them and drew the bishop aside. "Is the man here yet?"

"He may be," said Waleran. "Come to my house."

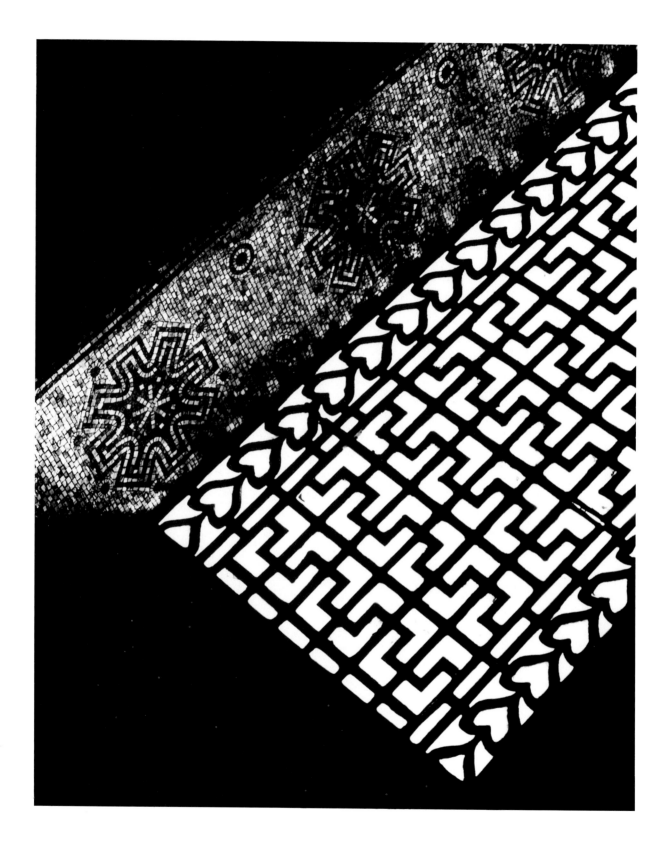

It was two years since the first cracks had appeared, and Jack had not found a solution to the problem. Worse still, identical cracks had appeared in the first bay of the nave. There was something crucially wrong with his design. The structure was strong enough to support the weight of the vault, but not to resist the winds that blew so hard against the high walls.

He stood on the scaffolding far above the ground, staring close-range at the new cracks, brooding. He needed to think of a way of bracing the upper part of the wall so that it would not move with the wind.

He reflected on the way the lower part of the wall was strengthened. In the outer wall of the aisle were strong, thick piers which were connected to the nave wall by half-arches hidden in the aisle roof. The half-arches and the piers propped up the wall at a distance, like remote buttresses. Because the props were hidden, the nave looked light and graceful.

He needed to devise a similar system for the upper part of the wall. He could make a two-story side aisle, and simply repeat the remote buttressing; but that would block the light coming in through the clerestory—and the whole idea of the new style of building was to bring more light into the church.

Of course, it was not the aisle as such that did the work: the support came from the heavy piers in the side wall and the connecting half-arches. The aisle concealed these structural elements. If only he could build piers and half-arches to support the clerestory *without* incorporating them into an aisle, he could solve the problem at a stroke.

❖

There was a stiff breeze up here, although at ground level it had hardly been noticeable. Jack looked down. If he fell from here he would land on the lean-to roof of the aisle alongside the transept. He would probably die, but it was not certain. He walked to the crossing and stood where the roof suddenly ended in a sheer drop. If the new-style cathedral was not structurally sound, and Aliena was leaving him, he had nothing left to live for.

Her decision was not as sudden as it seemed, of course. She had been discontented for years—they both had. But they had got accustomed to unhappiness. Winning back Earlscastle had shaken Aliena's torpor, and reminded her that she was in charge of her own life. It had destabilized a situation that was already unsteady; rather in the way that the storm had caused the cracks in the cathedral walls.

He looked at the wall of the transept and the roof of the side aisle. He could see the heavy buttresses jutting out from the wall of the side aisle, and he could visualize the half-arch, under the roof of the aisle, connecting the buttress to the foot of the clerestory. What would solve the problem, he had thought just before Philip had distracted him this morning, was a taller buttress, perhaps another twenty feet high, with a second half-arch leaping across the gap to the point on the wall where the cracks were appearing. The arch and the tall buttress would brace the top half of the church and keep the wall rigid when the wind blew.

That would probably solve the problem. The trouble was, if he built a two-story aisle to hide the extended buttress and the secondary half-arch, he would lose light; and if he did not . . .

If I don't, he thought, so what?

He was possessed by a feeling that nothing mattered very much, since his life was falling apart; and in that mood he could not see anything wrong with the idea of naked buttressing. Standing up here on the roof, he could easily picture what it would look like. A line of sturdy stone columns would rise up from the side wall of the aisle. From the top of each column, a half-arch would spring across empty space to the clerestory. Perhaps he would put a decorative pinnacle on top of each column, above the springing of the arch. Yes, that would look better.

It was a revolutionary idea, to build big strengthening members in a position where they would be starkly visible. But it was part of the new style to show how the building was being held up.

Anyway, his instinct said this was right.

The more he thought about it, the better he liked it. He visualized the church from the west. The half-arches would look like the wings of a flight of birds, all in a line, just about to take off. They need not be massive. As long as they were well made they could be slender and elegant, light yet strong, just like a bird's wing. Winged buttresses, he thought, for a church so light it could fly.

I wonder, he thought. I wonder if it would work.

A gust of wind suddenly unbalanced him. He teetered on the edge of the roof. For a moment he thought he was going to fall to his death. Then he regained his balance and stepped back from the edge, his heart pounding.

Slowly and carefully, he made his way back along the roof to the turret door, and went down.

He reached the top of the street
and turned into the priory close; and there,
before his eyes, was the reason for the rise
of Kingsbridge and the decline of Shiring: the
cathedral.

It was breathtaking.

The immensely tall nave was supported by
a row of graceful flying buttresses. The west
end had three huge porticos, like giants'
doorways, and rows of tall, slender, pointed
windows above, flanked by slim towers. The
concept had been heralded in the transepts,
finished eighteen years ago, but this was the
astonishing consummation of the idea. There
had never been a building like this anywhere
in England.

The market still took place here every
Sunday, and the green in front of the church
door was packed with stalls. William dis-
mounted and left Walter to take care of the
horses. He limped across the green to the
church: he was fifty-four years old, and heavy,
and he suffered constant pain from gout in
his legs and feet. Because of the pain he was
more or less permanently angry.

The church was even more impressive
inside. The nave followed the style of the
transepts, but the master builder had refined
his design, making the columns even more
slender and the windows larger. But there
was yet another innovation. William had
heard people talk of the colored glass made
by craftsmen Jack Jackson had brought over
from Paris. He had wondered why there was
such a fuss about it, for he imagined that a
colored window would be just like a tapestry
or a painting. Now he saw what they meant.

The light from outside shone through the colored glass, making it glow, and the effect was quite magical. The church was full of people craning their necks to stare up at the windows. The pictures showed Bible stories, Heaven and Hell, saints and prophets, disciples, and some of the Kingsbridge citizens who had presumably paid for the windows in which they appeared—a baker carrying his tray of loaves, a tanner and his hides, a mason with his compasses and level. I bet Philip made a fat profit out of those windows, William thought sourly.

The church was packed for the Easter service. The market was spreading into the interior of the building, as always happened, and walking up the nave William was offered cold beer, hot gingerbread and a quick fuck up against the wall for threepence. The clergy was forever trying to ban peddlers from churches but it was an impossible task. William exchanged greeting with the more important citizens of the county. But despite the social and commercial distractions William found his eye and his thoughts constantly drawn upward by the sweeping lines of the arcade. The arches and the windows, the piers with their clustered shafts, and the ribs and segments of the vaulted ceiling all seemed to point toward heaven in an inescapable reminder of what the building was for.

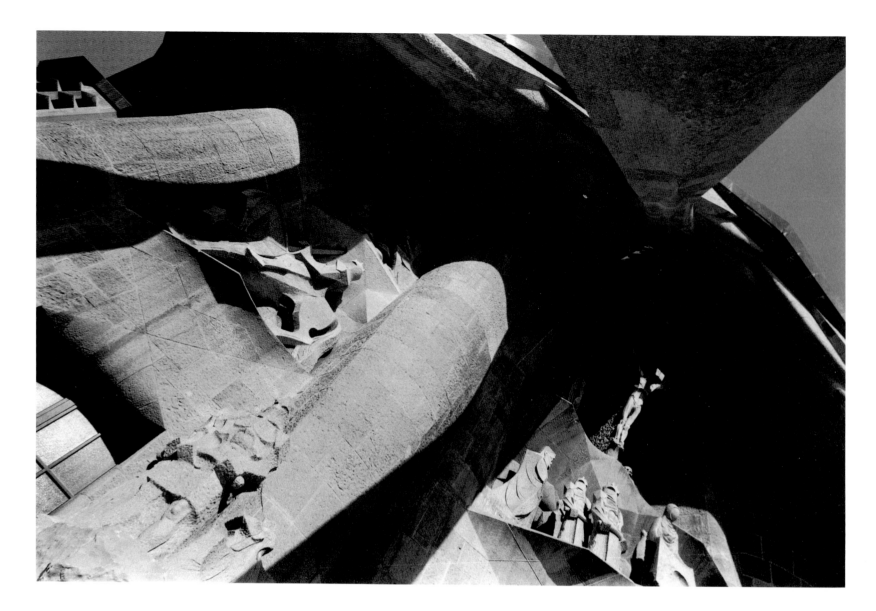

Index of Photographs

piece. This cathedral is perhaps one of the last Gothic-style buildings still under construction. From 1891 to April 1911, the original architects were Heins & LaFarge; from July 1911 to the present, Cram & Ferguson.

p. 11
SAINT ANNE DE BEAUPRÉ; Quebec, Canada
Up on a hill overlooking the St. Lawrence River, this is near the end of a series of outdoor sculptures depicting the Stations of the Cross. Shown here is a haunting crucifixion on Calvary. The present basilica was remade in stone, after a disastrous fire in 1926. It is a wonderful variation of the more traditional Romanesque design.

p. 13
WASHINGTON NATIONAL CATHEDRAL; Washington, D.C.
Although they are not at first apparent, this massive building is covered with grotesques and gargoyles. Each little, unassuming bump in this silhouette is in fact a detailed floral, geometric or human sculpture. No two are the same!

p. 15
COLOGNE CATHEDRAL; Cologne, Germany
Above the doors of the north transept, an example of the sculptural style of a family of artists—the Parlers. The tympanum over this doorway represents scenes of Satan rising into the air but brought back to earth by prayers.

p. 16
NOTRE-DAME DU CAP DE LA MADELEINE; Quebec, Canada
A pilgrimage site for thousands of visitors each year, this peaceful stream meanders throughout the grounds, with a bridge of giant rosary beads. In 1634 the first Jesuits arrived, including Jacques Buteux, who was later martyred by the Indians.

p. 17
OUR LADY OF CHARTRES CATHEDRAL; Chartres, France
Among the "Bibles in Stone" (cathedrals) of the world, Chartres clearly occupies a special place—whether for its famous stained glass windows, sculptures or architecture—including its position on the UNESCO World Heritage List of cultural and natural treasures.

With a total measurement of almost 27,000 square feet of stained glass, it represents arguably the greatest collection in the world. As stated so eloquently by Louis Gillet: "No prince ever owned such a book of Illuminations."

p. 18
CATHEDRAL OF SAINT JOHN THE DIVINE; New York City
These eerie figures on the pedestal of the central pillar—the trumeau—support a column over the archway. The four horseman represent Saints Matthew, Mark, Luke and John. The main figure is St. John.

p. 19
HOLY TRINITY ORTHODOX CATHEDRAL; Chicago, Illinois
Typically ornate, gilded and covered with religious icons, this small cathedral was designed by renowned Prairie School architect Louis Sullivan.

p. 20
URSULINE MUSEUM; Quebec, Canada
Shown here is a complex renovating program, with each detail of the altar being cleaned. As time shows its effect upon these magnificent creations, each must be carefully and tediously restored, by hand, even if aided by computer-enhanced imagery.

p. 23
THE CLOISTERS; New York City
The Fuentiduena Chapel was originally built on the Church of San Martín, north of Madrid, Spain. When the remainder of the church had fallen into disrepair, the Spanish government agreed to its reconstruction for the permanent collection of the Cloisters.

p. 24
THE CLOISTERS; New York City
As was typical of the framework of a monastery, the cloister was attached to the southern end of the church, providing a passageway, a processional walkway and a place for reading and meditation. The rich qualities typical of Romanesque designs are outstanding here in the Saint Michel de Cuxa Cloister.

p. 25
THE CLOISTERS; New York City
The Gothic Chapel features images installed in family burial sites, churches, or monasteries. Rather than intended as

portraits, they were likely symbols of the aristocratic and chivalric ideals of the times.

p. 26
CATHEDRAL OF AACHEN; Aachen, Germany
Missing from this view of the altar (seen from the upper floor) is the famed Barbarossa Chandelier, currently undergoing an exhaustive renovation. The chandelier was donated by emperor Barbarossa in honor of the Virgin Mary. It is said that the sixteen-sided chandelier was specially designed to match the octagonal form of the dome above. The two sets of eight plates represent the eight beatitudes and eight scenes from the life of Christ.

p. 28
ANCIENT SPANISH MONASTERY OF SAINT BERNARD; Miami, Florida
Originally built in Sacramenia, Spain, in 1133, this monastery was disassembled and shipped to the New World in 1925 by William Randolph Hearst. Although originally destined for his San Simeon estate, it became known as the World's Most Expensive Jigsaw Puzzle. Disassembled by suspicious customs inspectors, it was waylaid in Brooklyn, New York, for twenty-six years; after Hearst's death it was reconstructed in Miami in 1952.

p. 30
OUR LADY OF CHARTRES CATHEDRAL; Chartres, France
The total height of the roof is a towering 167 feet, allowing this view of the city and more. When a fire in 1836 destroyed the lead roof, the timbers were replaced with iron, and it was re-roofed in copper. The copper rapidly acquired the verdigris coloration, which harmonizes well with the gray of the Becheres stone.

p. 31
AMIENS CATHEDRAL; Amiens, France
Along the walkway of the cloisters, note the unusual intersecting arches of the ceiling. In 1206, Wallon de Sarton brought back Saint John's head during the Fourth Crusade, and the cathedral was needed as a place for this holy relic. With an eighteen-year period where construction stopped due to lack of funds, this beautiful, light cathedral was completed in only thirty years. It was here that, for the first time, mass-pro-

duction techniques were devised for cutting stones.

p. 32
CHRIST CHURCH CATHEDRAL; Montreal, Canada
An unusual Gothic church built in downtown Montreal, and surrounded by twentieth-century skyscrapers. A very popular shopping mall was constructed underneath the church, maintaining the traditional placement of the church at the crossroads of commerce.

p. 33
TRINITY EPISCOPAL CATHEDRAL; Miami, Florida
Located in central Miami, in addition to its stunning windows, and colorful mosaics, the cathedral contains dozens of exquisite hand-embroidered fabrics, depicting biblical scenes and tales.

p. 34
URSULINE MUSEUM; Quebec, Canada
Built into the altar can be seen small relics of saints and other religious figures. The museum, located within the walls of the old monastery, displays French and Canadian paintings, cabinet-making from the Louis XII era, seventeenth and eighteenth century sculptures and silver- and goldsmithing.

p. 35
COLOGNE CATHEDRAL; Cologne, Germany
Frequently referred to as the greatest church facade in Christendom, the immense, towering "Dom" has a richly decorated interior as well as a detailed and intricate exterior. Seen here is a detail from the huge bronze doors of the west facade.

p. 36
IL DUOMO; Milan, Italy
The Cathedral was built as a completion of Gian Galeazzo Visconti's desire to put Milan on the map of international framework. Rather than building in a "traditional" style, Visconti's use of Candoglian marble pushed the building toward its international stature. Milan soon became the link between the North and the culture of central Italy.

p. 37
THE CLOISTERS; New York City
A twentieth-century museum designated specifically for works created in

the Middle Ages, the Cloisters was made possible by a generous gift from John D. Rockefeller, Jr. He helped to provide the building, the hilltop setting and the acquisition of the magnificent George Grey Barnard collection of medieval art and architecture.

p. 38

RHEIMS CATHEDRAL; Reims, France
With a well-proportioned nave, the cathedral interior resembles a slender, elegant upturned ship's hull. Built with the influence of Chartres, Rheims Cathedral is presented in three stages: a series of large archways; quadruple arcading in the triforium; and slender lancet windows. This marks the first time the entire area is split up by fine tracery rather than ponderous, heavy lines.

p. 39

CATHEDRAL OF SAINT JOHN THE DIVINE; New York City
Along the back of the cathedral, several older statues show the effects of time and the elements. This cathedral is named after the author of the biblical book entitled The Revelation of Saint John the Divine—better known as the Book of Revelation.

p. 40

MOUNT ROYAL; Montreal, Canada
Sitting atop the highest hill of the city of Montreal, this modern cross replaces the original wooden cross built when its builder's prayers were answered when the town survived a flood. The hill site, Mount Royal, is the origination of the city's name—Montreal—settled in 1642 by a handful of French colonists.

p. 41

CATHEDRAL OF SAINTS PETER AND PAUL; Providence, Rhode Island
This image is an accidental—and lucky—double-exposure, showing the central crucifix with a detail of a gold-edged fish (symbolic of the Lord), appearing on the altar. The main altar is made of a rich green Vert d'Issorie, an unusual marble quarried in the French Alps.

p. 42

GLASTONBURY ABBEY; Glastonbury, England
The well-preserved ruins of an early medieval monastery. Local lore tells us

that this abbey was destroyed by Henry VIII, as part of his retaliation for the church's refusal to allow him to remarry yet again. Of special note is the kitchen, housed in an octagonal vault.

p. 43

SALISBURY CATHEDRAL; Salisbury, England
Near the main entrance to the nave, another gargoyle, showing the effects of about a thousand years passing through its mouth. The Cathedral houses the oldest existing clock in England, arguably the earliest working clock in the world. Completed by about 1386, it was originally housed in the bell tower, where the hourly notes were struck on the bells.

p. 44

SAINT ANNE DE BEAUPRÉ; Quebec, Canada
A statue of Saint Anne sits atop the large organ in the lower chapel of the basilica. The basilica combines traditional Romanesque grandeur with modern arts, all in the best of materials—marble, granite, mosaic, hand-carved wood and stained glass—exhibiting fine Canadian craftsmanship.

p. 45

IL DUOMO; Milan, Italy
The Cathedral was likely begun by 1386 by Archbishop Antonio da Saluzzo. The digging of the system of canals from Porta Ticinese to the Piazza Santo Stefano was due to the building of the Cathedral, thereby providing free transportation of the bright, white marble from Candoglia.

p. 47

ANCIENT SPANISH MONASTERY OF SAINT BERNARD; Miami, Florida
A beautiful formal garden, with such statues as Saint Anthony, allows the visitor to peacefully stroll and reflect amid the cityscape of Miami. The site was a nursery before the Monastery was reconstructed here and nearly 1,000 plants and trees of various types remain.

p. 48

TRINITY EPISCOPAL CATHEDRAL; Miami, Florida
As the viewer gazes heavenward, he or she is greeted with a heavenly sight: a beautiful, golden mosaic with angels bursting through the clouds and sun.

p. 51

BASILICA OF THE NATIONAL SHRINE OF THE IMMACULATE CONCEPTION; Washington, D.C.
A sorrowful sculpture depicting the Mother's anguish over the death of her Son greets the visitor at the entrance to the lower chapel of this Roman Catholic National Shrine. In the stained glass, art, architecture and mosaics, the history of the American Catholic devotion to the mother of Jesus can be found throughout the Shrine.

p. 52

CATHEDRAL OF SAINT JOHN THE DIVINE; New York City
With the knowledge that many of the world's greatest cathedrals may take a lifetime to build, it is likely that many lifetimes will be needed to conserve and preserve their wonders. Set on a thirteen-acre close, Saint John's is the largest Gothic cathedral in the world.

p. 55

WASHINGTON NATIONAL CATHEDRAL; Washington, D.C.
A detail of one of the thousands of small ornamentations and embellishments. This one, along the north transept, is at the bottom of a window and could easily be overlooked as an undistinguished floral pattern.

p. 56

URSULINE MUSEUM; Quebec, Canada
This gold-leaf angel is one of the details being carefully restored. In 1639, three Ursuline nuns from France arrived in Qubec. The Convent houses artifacts covering 120 years of French rule, and presents a historical overview of the French colony during this period.

p. 57

CATHEDRAL OF SAINT JOHN THE DIVINE; New York City
While only a somewhat primitive wooden carving on the end of the pew, this sort of charming detail abounds in many of the larger cathedrals. These are medieval choir stalls, relocated to Saint John's.

p. 58

NOTRE-DAME DE BONSECOURS; Quebec, Canada
This small cathedral was built as a remembrance for sailors and overlooks the St. Lawrence River in the heart of Montreal. The sailors' chapel is deco-

rated with many ex-votos—including some ship models given by seamen after their rescue.

p. 59

SAINT PATRICK'S CHURCH; Miami, Florida
A small church with mission-style adobe construction sits close to the Atlantic Ocean and is guarded by this lion with a Bible and a series of pelican figures perched overhead.

p. 61

WELLS CATHEDRAL; Wells, England
A view of the central nave, looking from the west end toward the Rood in the east. Note the unusual "scissors-arches." This church, along with all others in the kingdom, was closed by the Pope in 1209, due to his quarreling with King John. Work resumed with the overall concept in place; however, a skilled eye can find slight variations in the size of building stones and the foliage details atop capitals.

p. 62

OUR LADY OF CHARTRES CATHEDRAL; Chartres, France
This immense church, designed to accommodate large crowds, is the work of an unknown master. The magnificent flying buttresses, both powerful and delicate, are a wonderful example of the desired perfection of High Gothic.

p. 63

RHEIMS CATHEDRAL; Reims, France
The unusual help given to Caesar by the tribe of the Remi during his conquests assisted in making this city the most important in the region. It has maintained that position, being the site of over twenty-five coronations, from Louis VIII the Lion in 1223 to Charles VII, led by Joan of Arc, in 1429 through 1825 with Charles X.

p. 64

CATHEDRAL OF BARCELONA; Barcelona, Spain
As one of many smaller, regional cathedrals, these Spanish Gothic churches were simpler, more elegant buildings, uniform in style. In this manner the churches satisfied the needs at the local level, while avoiding any importation of French copies.

p. 65

NOTRE-DAME DE BONSECOURS; Quebec, Canada

Upon entering the chapel, the visitor will notice several golden and bejeweled hand-crafted boats hanging from the ceiling to recall the naval patrons of this church or as an offering to Our Lady for a rescue at sea.

p. 66

SAINT JOSEPH'S ORATORY OF MOUNT ROYAL; Montreal, Canada
Perhaps the most dynamic, forceful and elegant Stations of the Cross can be found on the wandering and escalating grounds of the Oratory. They represent the completion of a dream by the founder, Brother André. Models for the sculptures were by the Canadian artist Louis Parent and were carved by the Italian sculptor Ercolo Barbieri.

p. 67

CATHEDRAL OF SAINTS PETER AND PAUL; Providence, Rhode Island
A fine example of the Rose Window, here found in a small cathedral in the States, but an almost universal symbol found to a larger degree in European cathedrals. This West Rose Window presents scenes from the life of Our Lady, from the Annunciation to the Assumption, with the dominant color blue, that of the Blessed Mother.

p. 68

WASHINGTON NATIONAL CATHEDRAL; Washington, D.C.
A quieting example of the immense central nave. The view is from the upper balcony between the Saint Peter tower and the Saint Paul tower, looking toward the altar and choir.

p. 69

SAINT ANNE DE BEAUPRÉ; Quebec, Canada
While the Immaculate Conception is a universal and basic tenet of the Roman Catholic religion, this is an extremely rare acknowledgment of Mary's pregnancy, created in a somewhat primitive wooden sculpture with mission-style coloration. Along the same chapel are incredible ceiling mosaics, some of the best in this century.

p. 70

AMIENS CATHEDRAL; Amiens, France
As the local citizens so respected their cathedral, during the Revolution, the church was harmed amazingly little. The one area of abuse was in the bas-reliefs about the life of Saint Firmin. Again in

the two World Wars, it remained almost entirely untouched, with only an errant couple of shells hitting nearby, with little damage, in March 1918.

p. 71

SAINT JOSEPH'S ORATORY OF MOUNT ROYAL; Montreal, Canada
Sunlight streams through the stained glass window, falling upon the marble wall. The dome of Saint Joseph's stands like a beacon above the city of Montreal, with a profile which soars over 500 feet above street level.

p. 72

WASHINGTON NATIONAL CATHEDRAL; Washington, D.C.
This ancient tapestry depicts the slaying of the giant Goliath by David. The Cathedral is roughly based on fourteenth-century English Gothic style. It uses flying buttresses to support the 150,000-ton building—with no steel reinforcement.

p. 73

NOTRE-DAME DU CAP DE LA MADELEINE; Quebec, Canada
Construction of the modern basilica began in 1955 by the architect Adrien Dufresne. The dome stands 125 feet high with a seating capacity of 1660. The stained glass windows by the renowned Dutch artist Jan Tillemans, O.M.I., are unique in North America.

p. 75

RHEIMS CATHEDRAL; Reims, France
On the nave's side walls, the architectural design reaches perhaps its peak, where the builder created the bracing, robust arches with elegance. The solution was to double the number of flying buttresses while slimming them down. Over the buttresses, telamones hold the cornice of a gallery that hides the gutters; and gargoyles drain off water at each buttress.

p. 76

IL DUOMO; Milan, Italy
A marvel of white marble, huge and ethereal, covered with carvings, statues and belfries, should be seen in the light of the setting sun for full effect. The cathedral is adorned with 135 pinnacles and many other white marble statues. They can be viewed first-hand by going up to the roof, open to visitors 9 A.M. to 4 P.M. daily.

p. 78

IL DUOMO; Milan, Italy
How glorious that Cathedral is! worthy almost of standing face to face with the snow Alps; and itself a sort of snow dream by an artist architect, taken asleep in a glacier!—Elizabeth Barrett Browning

p. 79

NOTRE-DAME BASILICA; Montreal, Canada
An ornate woodcarving in black walnut at the base of the spiral staircase to the pulpit. The two figures represent the two prophets Ezekiel and Jeremiah. Carved from 1883 to 1885 by Philippe Hebert and designed by architect Victor Bourgeau.

p. 80

WASHINGTON NATIONAL CATHEDRAL; Washington, D.C.
An example of old-world craftsmanship and wit, this gargoyle, a clever rendering of the stonecarver, holds hammer, chisel and tools. The cathedral is 83,012 square feet, took eighty-three years to complete and cost approximately $65 million, all in private donations.

p. 82

RHEIMS CATHEDRAL; Reims, France
A view through the tower window. The Kings Gallery on the south tower contains sixty-three statues, with an average weight of four to five tons each and over four yards tall. This collection of kings reminds us of Reims's position in the anointing of kings, the earthly vicars of God.

p. 84

CATHEDRAL OF SAINT JOHN THE DIVINE; New York City
This sculpture in the plaza adjacent to the cathedral provides a foreground and foreshadowing of the seemingly endless construction and refurbishing necessary on such immense, complex buildings. The statue is the Peace Fountain, by Greg Wyatt, sculptor-in-residence.

p. 85

IL DUOMO; Milan, Italy
The Cathedral is an awful failure. Outside the design is monstrous and inartistic. The over-elaborated details stuck up high where no one can see them; everything is vile in it; it is, however, gigantic as a failure, through its great size and elaborate execution.—Oscar Wilde

p. 86

TEMPLO EXPIATORIO DE LA SAGRADA FAMILIA; Barcelona, Spain
From the mind of Catalan Modernist Antonio Gaudi y Cornet. He was a great sculptor with a legacy of daring forms of art. He is the heir of the medieval craftsmen who made last-minute decisions, while they were actually at work.

p. 87

SAINT JOSEPH'S ORATORY OF MOUNT ROYAL; Montreal, Canada
This is a somewhat primitive wooden sculpture of Adam. It is housed in the museum, two stories below the basilica of the Oratory and appears with a parallel carving of Eve.

p. 88

BASILICA OF THE NATIONAL SHRINE OF THE IMMACULATE CONCEPTION; Washington, D.C.
Deeply carved into its clean, white exterior, these larger-than-life carvings of Saints Simon, Matthew, Michael, et al., appear on both sides of the main entrance and run from ground level heavenward to the top of the building. In 1990, His Holiness Pope Paul II named the Shrine a minor basilica, a special designation given only to those churches noted for their antiquity and historical significance or as a center of worship.

p. 89

THE CLOISTERS; New York City
This is a detail of a larger piece depicting the death of Christ, carved in wood. The overall woodcarving possesses a large number of figures with delicate and unusual positioning of the hands.

p. 90

NOTRE-DAME BASILICA; Montreal, Canada
One of the most ornate and beautiful altars in North America, it is entirely plated with gold, set off by crystal blue (the color of Our Lady) accents. This masterpiece altar, built in 1875, is the design of Canadian architect Victor Bourgeau and enlivened by the famous sculptor Bouriche, from Anjou.

p. 91

NOTRE-DAME DE VICTOIRE; Montreal, Canada
This small church possesses the altar which seems to be made of solid gold

and has a small museum in the upstairs section, allowing visitors both an informative stopover and unparalleled views of the St. Lawrence River. The first chapel was erected here in 1657 under the auspices of Marguerite Bourgeoys, the founder of the Congregation of Notre Dame.

p. 92
AMIENS CATHEDRAL; Amiens, France
The Cathedral has a nave of six bays; a transept of which each arm has three bays; a choir of four bays and an ambulatory of seven parts with each having a corresponding radiating chapel. Its longest dimension is 476 feet compared to 426 feet in Paris and Chartres; and a height in the central nave of 139 feet compared to 121 in Chartres, 124 in Reims and 115 in Paris.

p. 93
CHURCH OF SAINT LAWRENCE; Île d'Orléans, Quebec, Canada
A small church, crafted in wood, which possesses a most intriguing and playful ceiling. In 1759, the English invaded the village under the command of General Wolfe. The fleeing parishioners took all of the church ornaments but a note left on the church door, signed by the priest, said: "It would have wished . . . that you could have arrived sooner so as to taste the vegetables . . . from my garden, that have all gone to seed."

p. 94
SAINT JOSEPH'S ORATORY OF MOUNT ROYAL; Montreal, Canada
This magnificent stone sculpture, showing the nailing to the cross, is part of the Stations of the Cross on the grounds of the Oratory. A procession through the Stations is generally held around dusk, and as seen here with the sun setting behind it, the sculpture seems to radiate with a self-contained light. The remarkable illumination of the statues was designed by a French master, Jean D'Orsay, who had previously lit historical monuments in Paris and Versailles.

p. 95
CHURCH OF SAINT PETRONILLE; Île d'Orléans, Quebec, Canada
An amazing statue of Christ, arms held heavenward, as if receiving a blessing from above. Note the single spire of the church in the background. The island is known for its strong religious

tradition, and a long list of priests and nuns from virtually all of the first families.

p. 96
THE CLOISTERS; New York City
A playful yet fearsome scene, carved at the capital of a column. As a reaction to this sort of robust, grotesque carving, more naturalistic floral patterns can be seen in the late thirteenth-century Bonnefont Cloister, from a strict ascetic Cistercian monastic order.

p. 97
CATHEDRAL OF SAINT JOHN THE DIVINE; New York City
A life-size prone sculpture of a shrouded body reaching heavenward, in the southern side of the central nave. This is the Auschwitz Holocaust Memorial, by Elliott Offner, dedicated May 30, 1978. It is one of three memorials in the mission bay, all related to acts of genocide in the twentieth century.

p. 98
IL DUOMO; Milan, Italy
The architect first mentioned for his lead model of the Cathedral in The Annales is Anechino de Alemania (February 9, 1387). However, the initiation of the project seems to belong to Simone da Orsenigo (December 6, 1387), the lead engineer, in collaboration with other local architects. The museum currently houses two separate original drawings of the building, both by Antonio di Vincenzo. Upon close examination, both drawings show differences from the actual building—notably a triple nave and a wider transept.

p. 99
OUR LADY OF CHARTRES CATHEDRAL; Chartres, France
The Chapelle Vendôme (originally fifteenth century) has two interesting newer additions. In 1791 two of the original windows lost their glass and were replaced after World War II. In the southern arm sits the window of Saint Fulbert, donated by the architects of America in 1954, and in 1971 Germany donated the window of Reconciliation in the northern arm.

p. 100
RHEIMS CATHEDRAL; Reims, France
The foundation of the current cathedral was laid on May 6, 1211, by Archbishop Aubry de Humbert. By its completion in 1275, the church construction had been

under the direction of four architects—master craftsman Jean d'Orbais, Jean de Loup, Gauchier de Reims and Bernard de Soissons—all of whom are represented in stones at the four corners of the nave.

p. 101
UNITY TEMPLE; Chicago, Illinois
This very unusual design in concrete bears the signature of one of the greats of American architecture—it was the first commission of Frank Lloyd Wright, seen perhaps at the very beginning of his Prairie School of architecture. It is a church without any steeple, nave or tower. As Wright stated: "Let us abolish in the art and craft of architecture . . . any symbolic form whatsoever. . . . Why not, then, build a temple, not to God in that way . . . but build a temple to man, appropriate to his uses . . ."

p. 102
CHRIST CHURCH CATHEDRAL; Montreal, Canada
The tall spire of the church is reflected in the adjacent modern high-rise office building. In order to maintain and repair the church, it was moved a few feet to allow for the construction of its neighbor, which has architectural characteristics resembling the church's, albeit with modern interpretation.

p. 103
TRINITY CHURCH: Boston, Massachusetts
This view of the spire of Trinity Church, seen here contrasted with an adjacent high-rise, shows the church's precarious position amid the sprawl of downtown Boston. As the church fronts three separate streets, the tower was chosen as the main feature, rather than being an inconvenient addition to the church, a typical Auvergnat solution.

p. 104
SAINT JOSEPH'S ORATORY OF MOUNT ROYAL; Montreal, Canada
The interior of the basilica was designed by Canadian architect Gerard Notebaert with furnishings by decorator Robert Prevost and mosaics by the Labouret Studios of France. On special occasions almost 12,000 standees have fit within its walls.

p. 105
IL DUOMO; Milan, Italy
Begun in 1386, the building was finally brought to a rapid completion by an

impatient Napoleon between 1805 and 1813. The Milanese expression *lungo come la fabricca del Duomo* refers to something that seems interminable.

p. 106 (top)
SAINT PATRICK'S CHURCH; Miami Florida
Built in the mission style of adobe and clay tiled roof amid coastal palm trees. The pelican perched alongside the main entrance seems appropriately placed.

p.106 (bottom)
THE CLOISTERS; New York City
Ancient stained glass window, probably dating from the twelfth century. Stained glass windows, with scenes from Christian and Hebrew stories, provided an important teaching function.

p. 107 (top)
SAINT NICHOLAS UKRAINIAN CATHOLIC CATHEDRAL; Chicago, Illinois
A unique frosted and lead-glass window, with a typical Eastern Orthodox icon, the multi-winged angel. The church is modeled after the Cathedral of Saint Sophia in Kiev, a multi-domed, eleventh-century wonder. This cathedral has thirteen domes, one each for Christ and his twelve apostles.

p. 107 (bottom)
COLOGNE CATHEDRAL; Cologne, Germany
Prior to World War II, many of the Cathedral's medieval and eighteenth-century stained glass windows were removed to safety. Unfortunately, from 1942 to 1945, the Cathedral was damaged heavily by fourteen bombs and air mines, in addition to shells and incendiary devices, causing thirteen arches to collapse. By 1948 it had been restored under Cathedral architect Willy Weyres.

p. 108
CATHEDRAL OF BARCELONA; Barcelona, Spain
As was typical of this era in Spanish religious architecture, the facades remained almost fortress-like in their somber decoration. Generally, there is only a single nave and if there are aisles, they are all of the same height, with slight columns and barely any decoration.

p.109
SAINT NICHOLAS UKRAINIAN CATHOLIC CATHEDRAL: Chicago, Illinois
This immense stained glass, round chan-

delier hangs from the dome, accentuated by repeated circular, octagonal and hemispherical arches. The interior of the cathedral was renovated by Boris Makarenko, an expert in Ukrainian Byzantine painting; the mosaics were designed by Makarenko and completed in Italy; the stained glass windows were created by the Munich Studio.

p. 110
CHURCH OF SAINT LAWRENCE; Île d'Orléans, Quebec, Canada
This small island community has always been a maritime and agricultural center, in addition to being a popular summer resort. One of the main agricultural products is berries—all sorts. They are a must to see and taste while on the island!

p. 111
AMIENS CATHEDRAL; Amiens, France
Over the centuries, Amiens Cathedral has been the site of many historical events: January 23, 1264—Saint Louis resolves a dispute between King Henri III and his barons; July 17, 1385—Charles VI of France weds Isabeau of Bavaria; May 8, 1550—King Henry II ratifies the Treaty of Outreau, giving Boulogne back to France; June 7, 1598—A proclamation of peace, the Peace of Vervins with Spain by Cardinal Legate de Medicis; and June 7, 1625—King Louis XIII's sister, Henriette de France, is married to Charles I of England.

p. 112-113 (top)
SAINT JOSEPH'S ORATORY OF MOUNT ROYAL; Montreal, Canada
A triptych of the nativity scene, with life-size statues. This is found in the museum of the Oratory in the lower level. The Oratory boasts a large collection of exhibits about the life of Saint Joseph—almost 300 in all.

p. 112 (bottom)
RHEIMS CATHEDRAL; Reims, France
Included among the treasures of the Cathedral are Charlemagne's talisman, taken from Napoleon I; the royal robes of Charles X's coronation; the chalice of the kings of France; and the vessel of Saint Ursula, offered to the church by Henry III.

p. 114
BOND CHAPEL; Chicago, Illinois
Dozens of tiny figurines, with no apparent structural purpose, adorn the top of the chapel, seen here with a complex pattern of crisscrossing vines. This gem of the Gothic Revival style is connected to the Divinity School. The figurines include griffins, dragons, demons and imps.

p. 115
GLASTONBURY ABBEY; Glastonbury, England
Although the abbey is currently in fairly good condition, for many years it was ignored and allowed to fall into disrepair. Due to the dearth of stones for building in the area, history tells us that many of the original stones of the abbey were, over the years, taken by the locals to use on their own construction projects.

p. 116
CATHEDRAL OF AACHEN; Aachen, Germany
The village is named after the renowned waters of its hot springs, a name that can be traced back to the Latin word for *water*. Charlemagne chose this site as his favorite due to its strategic position in his empire, as well as its warm mineral springs. The Cathedral contains the throne of Charlemagne, with six steps up, similar to King Solomon's throne.

p. 119
NATIONAL BASILICA; Washington, D.C.
This immense bronze sculpture shows Mary with child in the foreground and Joseph with donkey in the background, as affected by their exhausting travels. The expressions on Mary's face and the Christ Child's are reminiscent of those of a nursing mother and child who have both fallen asleep in bliss.

p. 120
HOLY TRINITY ORTHODOX CATHEDRAL; Chicago, Illinois
Although Louis Sullivan designed two other churches, this is the sole example which exists as he had intended. It stands as an excellent example of Sullivan's work, solving the interlocking demands of his own creative vision, economic conditions and religious ritual.

P. 121
ANCIENT SPANISH MONASTERY OF SAINT BERNARD; Miami, Florida
The unnatural growth of mangrove trees presents an unusual background for this delicate statue of the Virgin Mary. The statue was carved by an unknown sculptor in Cannes, France, and was donated to the church in the 1960s.

p. 122 (index)
TEMPLO EXPIATORIO DE LA SAGRADA FAMILIA; Barcelona, Spain
Proof of Gaudi's position as one of the last craftsmen in history is seen in the original pieces of furniture, mosaics and especially his wrought-iron objects, all of which exist in his many buildings, including this cathedral. He signals the end of the eclectic nineteenth-century architecture and leads the way to the contemporary, abandoning the restraints of the past.

back cover
See page 90.

ACKNOWLEDGMENTS

While, as always, there are many people without whom this book could not have happened, the following individuals and organizations deserve special mention. Many thanks to Mr. Ken Follett for kindly consenting to the use of his excerpts, as well as to his literary agent, Mr. Al Zuckerman, and to my literary agent, Jennifer Lyons, for making the project happen; to my favorite editor, Debbie Mercer, and Tom Nau at William Morrow.

I'm grateful for help on research, travel, contacts and untold other details: to the Canadian Tourist Office and Tourism Quebec; the Italian Government Travel Office; the British Government Tourist Office; the French Government Tourist Office; the Tourist Office of Spain; the Tourist Office of Germany; the Massachusetts Office of Tourism and the Greater Boston Convention and Visitors Bureau; the City of Chicago Office of Tourism; all for their help in arranging photography excursions to their respective cathedrals.

For assistance in transportation and logistics special gratitude is owed to Rail Europe and DER Tours of German Rail, for their real system of rail transportation, and to Hertz.

For exceptional accommodations, meals, logistics and business help thanks go to: in Canada, the Hotel Intercontinental of Montreal, the Loews le Concorde Hotel and Place Montcalm Restaurant in Quebec City; in the United States, the Midland Hotel, a small hotel with European charm in Chicago; in Britain, the No. 3 Restaurant & Hotel in Glastonbury, The Bury B&B in Cambridge, and the Little Mystole B&B in Canterbury, part of the Wolsey Lodges; in France, the Hotel Postillon and Les Marissons Restaurant in Amiens, the Hotel des Consuls and La Vigneraie Restaurant in Reims, and the Hotel de La Poste, Le Bistrot de la Cathédrale and Le Caveau de la Cathédrale restaurants in Chartres; in Germany, the Steigenberger Quellenhof Hotel, Spielcasino Internationales, the Ratskeller Restaurant and especially the Gala Restaurant in Aachen; and in Spain, the wonderful Hotel Colón in Barcelona.

For all the behind-the-scenes, critical work in the darkroom at Westwood Photo Productions in Mansfield, Massachusetts, thanks to Everett Winslow and Robert La Rose, Norman Christie, Christopher Winslow, Gary Deslaurier; and most specially to my old friend and assistant Richard McCaffrey, master technician.

For other technical help, I am grateful to my photographic assistants Edward Foley and Peter Rampson; for production assistance, thanks to Lilly Golden, Duncan Bock, Elizabeth Granatelli and my partner Will Balliett; and for research in the early stages of development, thanks to interns Shani Friedman and Caroline Anderson.

For irreplaceable help with photographic equipment, special thanks to Bill Pekala and the staff of Nikon Professional Services, and to Nikon Inc. for their splendid camera systems; also thanks to G.M.I. Photographic, importers of the great Bronica camera.

Finally, many thanks to all the people at the dozens of beautiful churches, abbeys, temples and cathedrals, first for the creation of such wonders and also for allowing me to partake of and document their beauty. Indeed, credit for the beauty of the many elements of this book, whether it be the architecture, stained glass, metalwork, masonry or sculpture, remains solidly in the hands of their individual creators and The Creator.